Steam's Last |

The summer of '69 on Northern Ireland Railways

By Michael R Stevenson

This book is dedicated to my wife Lorraine
who patiently put up with much of this story
in letterform many years ago.

Michael Stevenson is a lecturer in medical statistics at the Queen's University of Belfast, but the first data he ever collected was on locomotive performance on Northern Ireland Railways in the late 1960s. He is married to Lorraine and has two grown up daughters, Ruth and Laura.

6 5 4 3 2 1

© Michael R Stevenson
Newtownards 2000

Designed by Colourpoint Books,
Newtownards
Printed by ColourBooks

ISBN 1 898392 62 5

Colourpoint Books

Unit D5, Ards Business Centre
Jubilee Road
NEWTOWNARDS
County Down
Northern Ireland
BT23 4YH
Tel: 028 9182 0505
Fax: 028 9182 1900
E-mail: Info@colourpoint.co.uk
Web-site: www.colourpoint.co.uk

Photo Credits

All black and white photographs in this book were taken by JA Cassells, with the exception of the following:

CP Friel: photos on pages 8, 36 and 123
Ian Wilson: photo on page 39 (top)
Author: photo on page 114

Colour photographs are individually credited with the accompanying captions.

Front cover: NIR WT class 2-6-4T No 56 resting outside Coleraine shed on Easter Tuesday, 8 April 1969. This was one of only a few engines to carry the NIR logo.   *Richard Whitford*

Rear cover: No 53 departing from Portrush with the six coach 18.40 to Belfast on Easter Tuesday. In the background No 10 is preparing to take the ten coach 19.15. Portrush had four steam departures that evening.

Norman Johnston

Contents

Acknowledgements

To my daughters, Ruth and Laura, for listening patiently to Dad's stories and ultimately giving the smile test as a mark of suitability. To my mother and father, for their tolerance of my strange hours and even more unpredictable mealtimes. To Paul for joining me on many of these exploits.

To the engine-men and other servants of Northern Ireland Railways, many of whom have passed beyond this life. I have not mentioned details specifically. This is not to be disrespectful, for I do wish this book to be a celebration of their lives.

To the many enthusiasts who shared my passion for steam at this time and for the tales that they inspired. In particular, I would like to extend thanks to JA Cassells who, in addition to offering detailed comments on matters of historical fact, has provided so many of the photographs which support the text. Also thanks are due to Alex Lindsay, Ian Wilson and Charles Friel for valuable comments on matters of detail, or photographs, or both.

To the 'angel in blue' – I never knew her name!

I would also like to acknowledge the sources that have assisted me in producing this book. Principally these have been NIR timetables for 1969 (including the Easter and July Holiday Travel Arrangements); the *Belfast Telegraph;* RM Arnold's *Steam over Belfast Lough (*Oakwood Press, 1969) and *NCC Saga* (David & Charles, 1973); B Pender and H Richards' *Irish Railways Today* (Transport Research Associates, 1967); and an article by Roy G Chapman entitled 'Early Dieselisation in Ireland' *(Backtrack*, Vol 9, No 11, 1995, pp 572–9).

Foreword

This is unashamedly a book about trains – steam trains in particular. As such, it should be filed under railways/history. However, I have tried to write something more than just a plain railway history. In that sense it is an autobiography – of a 17-year-old growing up in a changing environment. So it is about my hopes and aspirations, fears and loves – or at least as I saw them then. The book also attempts to weave in non-railway events and how they affected me at the time. I do not know if the formula will work, but I have wanted to put down this text for some time and I am now glad I have.

Alternative Sound Track

Readers will note that songs that surrounded me during the summer of 1969 punctuate the book. Consequently these are almost entirely composed of pop chart material from that year. However, there are some latter day songs which perhaps paint aspects of the scene better, or have been suggested by the text. A list is provided below:

Song Title	Artist	Year
Summer of '69	*Bryan Adams*	*1984*
Girl on The Train	*Pete Atkin*	*1970*
Didn't Even Know Her Name	*Bread*	*1972*
Ol' '55	*Eagles*	*1974*
Hotel California	*Eagles*	*1976*
Man On The Moon	*REM*	*1992*
Wait	*Sarah McLaughlan*	*1994*
Stand by Me	*Oasis*	*1997*
Candle in the Wind (1997)	*Elton John*	*1997*

Glossary of Terms

AEC	Associated Equipment Company
BCDR	Belfast & County Down Railway
BUT	British United Traction
CIÉ	Coras Iompair Éireann
'Crockered start'	A term used where a driver is beckoned to slow after starting – perhaps because a passenger has attempted to board the moving train or a carriage door has not been closed properly.
DEMU	Diesel Electric Multiple Unit (see below *)
GNR	Great Northern Railway (of Ireland)
Jeep	The affectionate name by which the 2-6-4T engines were known. The name was a reference to their ease of handling. Built to the same specification as the 'W' class moguls, they thus took the letter classification 'WT'.
MED	Multi-Engined Diesel
MPD	Multi-Purpose Diesel
NCC	Northern Counties Committee (of the London Scottish and Midland Railway)
NIR	Northern Ireland Railways
RPSI	Railway Preservation Society of Ireland
SLNCR	Sligo Leitrim and Northern Counties Railway
UTA	Ulster Transport Authority

* There were three types of DEMU:
– 70-class or 'Hampshire' class, introduced in 1966 and withdrawn in 1985-86. These units were nicknamed 'Hampshires' because they were modelled on mechanically similar DEMUs operating on the Southern Region of British Railways but with UTA/NIR bodies.
– 80-class, introduced in 1974 and still in use. Similar in power to the 70-class, but with British Rail Mark 2 bodyshells.
– 450-class, introduced in 1986 but powered by reconditioned 70-class engines. These DEMUs have British Rail Mark 3 bodyshells.

Note
All engine and railcar numbers appear in italics throughout the text and in normal print in captions.

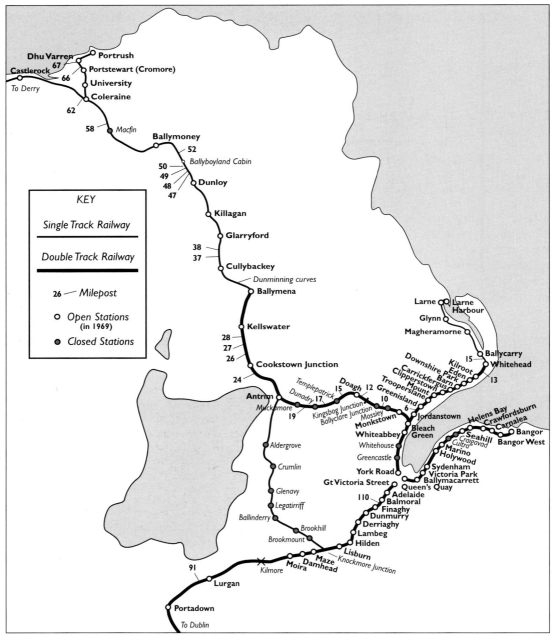

The Author's Journeys on NIR in 1969

Prologue

17.14 hrs: Thursday 23 January 1969

It's just after 5.00 pm on a Monday evening in January 1969, but since British Summer Time is in force, it is still daylight as I rush round to Platform 4 at Great Victoria Street (sited where Platform 3 in the rebuilt station lies). A four-car BUT set is preparing to leave on the 17.10 (Dunmurry, Hilden and all stations except 'the Maze' to Portadown). Out of the corner of my eye I see a very attractive young woman, stepping out briskly for the train, but other than to register that she is indeed pleasing to the eye, the event really should leave no further mark – no further mark that is, if I never see her again.

Three days later, on a rather grey but unseasonably mild evening, it's the same time, same place, same train, though a slightly different formation of railcars. Unusually for me, as I tended to travel at the front, I boarded the rear coach, and sat in the back facing window seat on the right hand (i.e. milepost) side of the coach. This coach was number *121*, a powered BUT double-ended unit, containing second class low-backed armchair seats. A few minutes later a woman got on board and sat down beside me – it was the same girl. The train started away close to time, the run out of Great Victoria Street being very standard stuff for this type of unit in a four-car formation. Opposite me sat a workman, his dress strongly suggesting that he worked in the building trade, and a colleague sat beside him. I can't remember if it was yet the custom to pay labourers on a Thursday evening, but this guy was rather the worse for drink. This was an unusual sight on NIR in the late 1960s and for a teatime train it was most unusual. He was rambling loudly to his friend about "the wife doesn't love me anymore". It's odd that when there is a scene in a public place, those not involved tend to look at each other, rather than directly at the scene maker. Also, given the somewhat anti-social behaviour, there would have been a degree of unease amongst the rest of the passengers – sufficient unease, perhaps, to make one feel more safe and more comfortable than usual with 'normal' travelling companions – as if I needed any further excuse to feel more comfortable about the person next to whom I was seated! Out of the corner of my eye I suddenly became aware of this lady momentarily turning her gaze to me, but I mistimed my response as she quickly turned away. Alone, I found myself, for just for a few seconds, staring at a cameo of the most beautiful face I had ever seen in my life. Blond-haired, blue-eyed, sophisticated, economical in movement, moreover just plain drop-dead gorgeous and I was spellbound – I was caught – I was check-mated as if forever. And so, at 17.14 on 23 January 1969, as a rush-hour commuter train scrambled past Adelaide halt, and as someone somewhere softly sang 'Well no-one told me about her...But it's too late to say I'm sorry...She's not there', I fell madly in love with the 'angel in blue'.

April 69

Saturday 5 April

In Northern Ireland an early Easter tends to be a meteorological disaster. Instead of idyllic scenes of new-born lambs basking in the sunshine, we get biting winds and horizontal sleet. I say this as a generality of course, and generalities can be broken. Fortunately, such was the case in 1969. The period before Easter had been uncommonly dry, and now the holiday weekend presented fine sunshine. So, as people woke up to the fact that winter was finally over, many decided that a few days away in hotels, boarding houses or indeed in the fast growing recreation of your own caravan at the seaside, was just what the doctor ordered. Many took their own cars, sitting for hours in traffic jams on what was a rather less developed road system than we boast today. But there were still large numbers who flocked to one of Belfast's three railway termini. If you wanted a weekend in Dublin, or maybe Greystones or Bray, you headed for Great Victoria Street. There, a train composed of coaches hauled by a diesel electric locomotive owned by the Irish Railway company, CIÉ, or perhaps one of Northern Ireland Railways new 'Hampshire units', would whisk you to you destination.

Maybe you couldn't afford to go so far afield, so the remedy was a day trip to Bangor. So you

(Continued on page 13)

General view of York Road shed in 1969. In the foreground 5 has just been turned. Ex-SLNCR 0-6-4T 27 Lough Erne *and two unidentified jeeps can also be seen.*

The rear of York Road shed on 15 January 1969 showing 2-6-4T No 6 at the ash pit with a set of 'failed' AECs in the background.

Norman Johnston

A view of 53 approaching Monkstown with the 09.25 to Portrush on 7 April 1969.

Richard Whitford

Jeep 56 approaching Portstewart (known locally as Cromore) with the 13.30 ex-Coleraine on 7 April 1969.
Richard Whitford

No 4 rescues a stricken MPD set later that day. The failed railcar is seen passing Dhu Varren halt.
Richard Whitford

No 10 passing Dhu Varren with the 19.15 to Belfast on 7 April 1969.

Richard Whitford

No 171, the preserved ex-GNR 4-4-0, heads towards Ballymena with the 10.25 special to Portrush on 8 April 1969. Although a preserved locomotive, 171 was on a company train, being 'run in' after overhaul.

Norman Johnston

Engines 56 and 171 on shed at Coleraine, 8 April 1969. The shed area is now occupied by an Ulsterbus garage.
Richard Whitford

Jeep 53 with a train of empty coaches coasts along Magilligan Strand as she approaches Downhill on 8 April 1969.

Norman Johnston

(Continued from page 8)

headed to Queen's Quay station, where a diesel multiple unit would run down the twelve miles or so to the seaside in under half-an-hour.

In both cases one thing was certain – you would not be transported to you destination by a steam train. The Great Northern section had ceased all steam operations from November 1966; while the loss of the Central line connection had ensured that the now self-contained Bangor line was devoid of steam from August 1965.

But if you headed to York Road station this was by no means a certainty. For York Road engine shed still boasted a fleet of nine mixed traffic 2-6-4 tank locomotives. British Railways had ceased all steam operations from 10 August the previous year, while in the Republic of Ireland CIÉ had ended steam hauled trains as early as 1963. So, the metals of the former Northern Counties Committee became the last standard gauge lines in the British Isles to have express and commuter hauled steam trains. The entire fleet, all of LMS 2-6-4 tank-engine design, were numbered in ascending order – *4, 5, 6, 10, 50, 51, 53, 55* and *56*. They are the true stars of this book, and all will feature in due course.

So if you had arrived at York Road to travel on the 11.45 diesel to Londonderry, changing at Coleraine for the branch train to Portrush, you would have encountered an interesting alteration to the usual schedule. Because of the increased traffic, the regular train was not carrying passengers for Portrush. Instead, a relief train had been provided, leaving at midday and running straight through to the north Antrim seaside town. This train, with a very modest load of five coaches, was in the hands of shed favourite engine number *4* with driver Rab Graham and fireman Gerry Phelan.

From York Road the first three miles of railway were along what was then called the lough shore. (The building of the M2/M5 motorway and much reclamation of land have served to erase from memory the fact that this was once shoreline.) Then the line climbs at a gradient of 1/89 for a mile to Whiteabbey station, where there is a short

Left to right: drivers Rab Graham and Willie Cameron and fireman Willie Graham.

easing, followed by almost five miles at a ruling gradient of 1/75. This brings us to Kingsbog Junction where there was a signal cabin and crossover, which enabled pilot engines to be detached from double-headed trains. The line then drops steadily to Antrim, with an easing through Templepatrick station.

Graham made an easy start out to Seaview (home to Crusaders football club) and then found progress along the lough shore hindered by a permanent way slack at Greencastle. At the foot of the bank at Whitehouse speed had only recovered to 34 mph. But *4* was handled so competently that we fell only fractionally below 30 mph at Monkstown and were away to 45 mph by the time we passed Kingsbog Junction. We then touched 64 mph, before a signal check at the crossing gates at Milepost 15 ruined the run down the hill. Not to be deterred, Graham had *4* away to

69 mph at Dunadry before easing for the Muckamore curves and the Antrim stop reached in just 30 m 44 s – without the permanent way slack and signal check this could easily have been a fine 27 minute run.

The line beyond Antrim rises for four miles to Milepost 26, then drops for the next two and a half miles and undulates much of the rest of the way to Ballymena. The final half mile is on rising ground, which is particularly useful in getting a swift start for trains travelling towards Belfast. Graham and 4 accelerated steadily up through Cookstown Junction, with the speed rising to 51 mph by Post 26, and then got away to 66 mph on the easier terrain, before stopping in Ballymena in a fine time of 14 m 30 s.

North of Ballymena, the line rises for nearly five miles to Dunminning, though there is an easing for about a mile south of Cullybackey station. Then the line encounters chicane reverse curves, drops into Glarryford and undulates across the marshland to Dunloy. Two miles north of Dunloy, the line curves and descends through Ballyboyland for the final five miles into Ballymoney. There is a short easing of the bank just past the site of the signal cabin. After replenishing the engine with water, taken from the tower at the north end of platform one, Graham made a spirited start up to Cullybackey, just shading 40 mph and stopping in under seven minutes. There we had a long stop, though it was not until the next stop at Dunloy that we actually had to cross an on-coming diesel. A speed of 41 mph before Dunminning, 60 mph at Glarryford and just over 13 minutes to Dunloy was smart work. Unfortunately, with the extra volume of traffic, Ballyboyland cabin and loop were 'switched in', which necessitated a hand tablet exchange, so we achieved just 54 mph before and 58 mph after the slack.

Yet another lengthy stop was made to await the arrival of the 12.30 multi-purpose diesel from Londonderry. The line on to Coleraine is fairly undulating, most notable features being a one-mile climb through Macfin station and a sharp descent for about a mile, after the line burrows under the main Belfast to Coleraine road (known

hereafter as the A26). Unfortunately, road widening was in progress and this required a strengthening of the bridge. Hence a permanent way restriction operated throughout the entire spring and summer of 1969. Graham and 4 managed 59 mph before Macfin and 58 mph before the restriction, without which a speed well into the mid or high 60s would surely have been recorded down past Windyhall housing estate.

The branch to Portrush climbs for the first mile toward University halt, then undulates through Portstewart, before finally plunging at 1/76 for the final mile through Dhu Varren and into the seaside terminus. Graham made a fine start out of Coleraine, exceeding 46 mph at Portstewart and through Dhu Varren in just over nine minutes, before a signal stop just outside Portrush dented progress. Notwithstanding the light load, this had been a fine start to the Easter weekend.

The number of people travelling had been swollen by a considerable number of enthusiasts, many of whom had purchased unlimited travel tickets for the princely sum of 50 shillings (£2.50). At Portrush we all detrained, hoping to find a friendly and considerate guard who would let us travel on 4's next train, which was actually rostered as an 'empty coaches' working. She was to proceed to Londonderry via Coleraine where she would be cleaned and the fire dropped. She would then stable at Derry until Monday, when she would be lit up early to provide motive power for an excursion train from the maiden city to Portrush. As the shed no longer had facilities to coal an engine, she would have to rely on the reserves of her 'high bunk'. Consequently a different engine would be required for the return working to Londonderry on Monday evening, with 4 returning to Belfast.

A friendly guard was indeed found and a further 40 steam miles assured. Empty coaches trains are not supposed to be worked hard, which renders all the more incredible the fact that Graham was doing 38 mph at Milepost 66 and 49 mph at University (passed in under nine minutes), before the usual signal check outside Coleraine hindered progress. We all had plenty of time for

A view of 4 from within the old Londonderry terminus, 5 April 1969.

some refreshment at Coleraine, while *4* was turned. So she worked bunk first both from Portrush to Coleraine and from Coleraine to Londonderry, but this meant that she would not need to be turned again to ensure a chimney first run on Monday morning. The line from Coleraine to Londonderry is 33½ miles of almost entirely level track. The line hogs the North Atlantic coast until Magilligan, and then it is never far away from Lough Foyle. A fine empty coaches run ensued, with 64 mph attained before Limavady Junction and 58 mph afterwards. We were into the maiden city in plenty of time to take some photographs, before catching the diesel back to Belfast. Also noted was an additional rake of six steam coaches that had been stabled at Derry throughout the winter. This had been the real reason for *4*'s light load today. On Monday she would be required to haul eleven coaches back to Portrush.

The 17.40 home was worked by six-car MPD set with a 'bogie van' attached. Cars *42*, *43*, *51* and *60* made up the motive power and suffice to say that for once an MPD set was fairly well behaved!

Easter Sunday 6 April

Easter Sunday and even steam engines deserve a day off! Even the steam-hauled Great Northern ballast train was cancelled. Instead, my brother Paul and I took the train to Bangor, while my father made the journey by car to visit my grandfather and aunt. Thirty years ago you could not get on a train at Lisburn, where we then resided, and travel straight through to Bangor. You had to travel into Great Victoria Street and then walk the mile to Queen's Quay for the next stage of the journey. We caught the 15.05 from Lisburn courtesy of a four-car BUT diesel set – strengthened by having a formation of three power units (*128*, *129* and *135*) to just one trailer. This should have resulted in very sharp running. That it did not was clearly due to at least one of the six engines being non-functional. I gave Paul some 'timing practice' and he confirmed that no more than 51 mph had been attained coming in from Finaghy. Whatever the problem, we were 11 minutes late into Great Victoria Street and had to trot briskly through the dank, foul-smelling subways that punctuated the route to Queen's Quay. The five-car multi-engined diesel set was well populated, but was in no better form that the BUT. Units *16*, *34* and *35* supplied the power. This set had had new four-speed gearboxes fitted. Managing only 51 mph before Holywood was dull and the uphill work was fairly weak too.

With the visit over, we returned on the 19.30 ex-Bangor, courtesy of a four-car set (with power units *17* and *24*). Uphill work was very weak, though 62 mph between Seahill and Holywood was probably more than the track could currently bear. We also failed to touch 50 mph between Holywood and Sydenham – a feat that the worst of the 450-class can occasionally emulate!

Easter Monday 7 April

I think if I could have two days to live over again, I would choose Easter Monday and Tuesday, 1969. The 'troubles' that would soon afflict us were but a phantom. If the trusty steam engines were on their last uppers – well it just didn't seem that way. The sun shone, God was in His heaven and through my eyes the blue angel radiated a pink-hued aurora!

Rab Graham, hero of Saturday, became superhero of Monday. NIR had initially deemed that just two excursions to Portrush would be steam hauled – one from Derry, in the hands of number *4* and one from Belfast, a nine coach affair leaving at 09.25 and stopping at Antrim only. This was assigned to the shed's number two engine – *53*. The second excursion was a diesel and was due to leave Belfast at 09.40 and run empty to Antrim where it would become the 10.15 to Portrush, making the usual array of intermediate stops. But the good weather had brought people out in droves. There was simply no way that the 09.40 and the third excursion at 10.25 could both be diesel-hauled. Consequently, a very clean *56* was despatched light engine to Antrim, where a rake of seven coaches, that clearly had not run all winter, was put back into action. The engine was in fine form, not so the coaches, but more about this later.

Had the shed been prepared in good time, *56* could have double headed *53* to Antrim. Such had been the arrangement on Easter Monday 1968,

when *50* and *55* had managed a breathtaking 80 mph through Dunadry.

The crew assigned to the 09.25 were driver Rab Graham, ably assisted by fireman Barney McCrory. We were seven minutes late away, Rab taking the lough shore very easily because of the permanent way restriction and attaining nothing more than 41 mph. But *53* was made to work fairly hard up through Monkstown (see page 9) and held a creditable 21 mph with her 300-ton load. With recovery to 36 mph by Kingsbog, Rab worked the engine steadily down the hill and we touched 70 mph before easing for the Muckamore curves. Thirty-two minutes to Antrim was no record, but without the slack much was in keeping with what would have passed for a half hour run – always reckoned as a good standard for a heavy train.

Even though this was the only train definitely rostered as steam, NIR had produced a diesel timing for the non-stop run to Portrush. The allowance was 15 minutes to pass Ballymena, a further 26 minutes on to Ballymoney, another ten minutes on to Coleraine (including the A26 bridge slack) and finally a 'recovery' 15 minute schedule over the branch – 66 minutes in all for the 46 miles. The one thing that was certain with a heavy steam train, was that we would have to add an extra stop at Ballymena for water. This we did in just two seconds under 16 minutes, after 44 mph through Cookstown Junction and 61 mph at Kellswater. At Ballymena, as Barney attended to *53*'s replenishment, big Graham beamed down from the cab, well satisfied with the engine's performance. And he had every right to be so, for he ran the next section to Portrush in a running time of just 50 minutes, despite a signal stop on the Portrush side of Coleraine. The start up to Cullybackey was one of the best I ever recorded with a big train – over 42 mph before the village and a fine hand tablet exchange taken at 40 mph. We 'hammered' on up to Milepost 38 at a steady 42–43 mph. Once onto the undulating section we shaded 55 mph at Glarryford and again before Dunloy, taking the hand exchange there at 41 mph. A fine 67 mph down Ballyboyland took us through Ballymoney in just under 26½ minutes. We then exceeded 61 mph both before and after Macfin. Then the bridge slack took its toll, but the time to pass Coleraine was still under 37 minutes. Even though Portstewart loop was switched in, thus requiring an additional hand tablet exchange (taken at 26 mph), we still managed 42 mph on the branch. So, despite two additional stops, a permanent way slack and three hand tablet exchanges, the 66-minute running time from Antrim to Portrush had been held. That we were now thirteen minutes late merely reflected the length of those stops. Quite simply, this was one of the finest crafted runs of the year and it was a delight to have participated.

The 09.25 was also rostered to work an 11.37 branch train back to Coleraine. One would have expected most of the nine coaches to be left behind at Portrush, but to clear the decks for the heavier than anticipated traffic still to come, the entire set formed the train. This turned out to be a prototype on how to work a heavy train up the 1/76 gradient out of Portrush. Graham, with *53* now running bunk first, was through Dhu Varren

in just over two minutes, accelerated to 35 mph by the top of the bank at Milepost 66 and then managed 46 mph after the hand tablet exchange at Portrush. Even a bad signal check after University could not stop nearly two minutes being knocked off the schedule of 15.

A resplendent *56* drifted in with the 10.15 from Antrim. The seven-coach load was an easy enough burden. But driver George Houston and fireman Gerry Phelan clearly had a problem that had cost them time. An acrid burning smell issued forth from an axle box in the second coach. The set that had not been used all winter was clearly prone to 'hot boxes' and speed had to be curtailed to deal with this. So he started briskly out of Coleraine and then did not exceed 37 mph on the branch. Even so, two minutes were regained by Portrush.

Once the passengers had detrained, the front two coaches were shunted into a siding and the remaining five made up a 13.10 empty coaches back to Coleraine. We had to slack to walking pace at Dhu Varren. The dry weather and spring sunshine had actually resulted in the grassy bank

No 4 arriving at Coleraine with the 11-coach 11.25 special from Londonderry to Portrush.

going on fire, presumably from a spark or cinder from a passing steam train! An easy run back to Coleraine ensued with nothing more than 39 mph.

Even if you hadn't got up early to go to the seaside, courtesy of one of the through excursions to Portrush, there was still the possibility of travelling on a Londonderry bound diesel and changing at Coleraine. Thus the 11.45 ex-York Road was well populated and very late and resulted in the 13.30 branch steam train being well patronised (see page 10). We had to slack at Portstewart to pass number *4* running light engine back to Coleraine. She had deposited her 11-coach train from Derry at Portrush. Otherwise we trundled along the branch at no more than 34 mph and arrived at Portrush some 22 minutes behind schedule. Number *56* was despatched light to Coleraine and a quiet afternoon ensued, basking in the moderately warm sunshine on the grassy slopes above Dhu Varren.

In the late afternoon, we were awakened from our slumbers to witness an unusual sight. An engine with a low bunk (number *4* and all of the remaining engines numbered in the 50s possessed high bunks that enabled greater mileage between coalings) was approaching Portrush with a long rake made up of every last steam coach that NIR possessed. The engine was number *10* and she would be the last low bunk engine ever to reach Portrush on a passenger working. Originally the extended bunk had been developed to permit the 'jeeps' to run to Dublin and back on a single load of coal – 225 route miles in all. Belfast to Londonderry plus three return trips on the Portrush branch amounted to about the same – 222 miles in all. For this reason *4* would be despatched to Belfast on the last excursion home, while *53* would take her place on the Derry bound excursion. Number *4* was fortunate in only having to deal with five coaches on the previous Saturday. On the other hand, *53* had been worked hard with nearly twice the load, and hence higher coal consumption. This would lead to some interesting developments the next day.

The first steam excursion to Belfast was booked out of Portrush at 19.15, with others

Jeep 56 seen just above Dhu Varren running light to Portrush to take up her evening duties.

No 10 preparing to leave with the 19.15 to Belfast. No 4 has been watered and 56 sits at the head of the 19.45. The author and Robert White in the first compartment are talking to Irwin Pryce (with glasses). Also clearly distinguishable are Drew Donaldson (looking out) and Mac Arnold with his coat (awaiting better things).

following at 19.30 and 19.45. This task was given to *10* with the troublesome rake of coaches that *56* had taken charge of that morning. The crippled coach had been parked in a siding at Portrush, so the load was now reduced to six. This was an easy prospect and the sight of ex-Great Northern man, Jimmy Donnelly, gave additional reason to cover this turn at least as far as the first stop in Ballymena. A moderately easy run along the branch (see page 11) produced a top speed of 45 mph, but then we were stopped by signals outside Coleraine. By the time we got under way again, we were already 11 minutes down on schedule, but time was more or less held on the way to Ballymena, despite the appearance of yet another coach with a hot axle bearing. Donnelly managed 53 mph before Ballymoney, sustained 32–33 mph over the worst part of the Ballyboyland bank and then ran the rest of the way up at a solid 38–39 mph. We just shaded 56 mph at Glarryford when the axle problem was detected, and we trundled down through Cullybackey keeping generally below 40 mph to reduce the degree of wear on the faulty bearing.

At Ballymena there was nothing else for it. The stricken coach had to be shunted into a siding and passengers huddled rather uncomfortably into the remaining five-coach train – all of which took time, as the remaining light of the day faded. It was almost five to nine before Donnelly got under way again – *10* and her light load starting out of Ballymena with near tube train acceleration. At the north end of the platform in the gathering gloom you could just see two oil lamps, in express train formation, on a locomotive halted at the outer home signal. Once the signal was released, *56* crept forward to the water column, bringing with her the nine-coach rake that *53* had entertained that morning.

I did not yet know it, but this would prove to be my last run with *56*. The delay had cost us a half hour, yet Paddy Dobbin, assisted by fireman Dave Smith, was in no hurry away – either he caught adverse signals or the engine primed badly after the delay. Despite this we recovered to gain 58 mph at Kellswater, held 55 mph over Milepost 26 and touched 63 mph before the stop in Antrim. The start out of Antrim was wonderful, with 50 mph at Muckamore, 42 mph over the worst part of the bank (at what today is the Airport Road crossing). We recovered to 45–46 mph through Templepatrick and looked set to hold above 40 mph over Kingsbog. But *56* tired a bit towards the summit, with a final minimum of 39 mph. A speed of 62 mph at Monkstown and a final time of 28½ minutes in from Antrim (after a signal check just outside the terminus) brought a very memorable and enjoyable day to a close. Paul and I eventually reached home about 23.15, after a run as far as Lambeg with the same faulty BUT unit featured in Sunday's exploits, and got just about enough sleep to get up and do it all again the next day!

Easter Tuesday 8 April

By 08.20 we were back at Lambeg station, waiting for the 08.15 from Lisburn – a six-car AEC diesel unit with power units *111*, *115*, *118* and *120*. After making the journey on foot to York Road, a decision had to be made. Two trains were rostered steam, but in fact three steam trains were eventually required. The first was˙ the 09.25, similar in formation to Monday, but with *4* and Willie Gillespie as engine and driver. Later that month the Railway Preservation Society of Ireland (RPSI) would host their most ambitious venture to date – the Cork tour. Two engines would be required – one jeep and the engine they currently rented from NIR – S-class *171* 'Slieve Gullion'. I stress the fact 'rented', for, on 8 April 1969, *171* was still technically the property of NIR and so this was the last time that a Great Northern engine worked a passenger train in 'company' days. For *171*, with a load of seven coaches, was rostered to work the 10.25 to Portrush (see page 11, lower). She had just completed a major overhaul at Harland and Wolff and working this train would help to 'run her in' before the big trip to Cork. The 10.15 ex-Antrim was supposed to be a diesel – but once again *56* was required. Today she would run effectively as a second excursion, leaving York Road at 09.40.

Most enthusiasts knew I was a Great Northern man at heart. They fully expected me to choose the trip with *171*. In particular, Norman Foster was pleasantly surprised when I explained that as *171* would be around for years to come, but *4* might not, I would be covering the first excursion. Indeed, if I had known then that *4* would be preserved, moreover had I known the fate that would shortly befall *56*, I would have chosen the latter on what turned out to be her last run to Portrush.

Driver WJ Gillespie and fireman Barney McCrory ran rather more tentatively to Antrim than Graham had done the· previous day. The permanent way slack out along the lough shore was strictly observed and we fell momentarily to 18 mph at Monkstown and a very easy downhill run produced nothing more than 61 mph, taking nearly 35 minutes to Antrim. But just when it looked like big Graham would walk away with the honours, Tuesday's team ran to Ballymena in just over 15 minutes, with an excellent 48–49 mph up to Milepost 26 and 62 mph at Kellswater. After taking water we made another good start up though Cullybackey, though Gillespie did not chance the hand tablet exchanges at quite the pace of the previous day. Nevertheless, 40 mph at Post 38 and 56 mph before Dunloy were creditable performances, even if we got no more than 61 mph down Ballyboyland nor 55 mph before Macfin. We'd lost a little time by Coleraine, but a sharp run along the branch with 41 mph before the Portstewart hand tablet exchange, meant that not even a final signal check could avoid a time of well under 51 minutes from Ballymena and arrival just eight minutes late. For the second day in succession the 66-minute running time from Antrim had been kept.

Sadly steam was not required on the 11.37 local – this was given to a three-car 'Hampshire' set (with power unit *74*). We stopped at Portstewart where I had time to photograph *56* on the second excursion running considerably earlier than on Monday. At Coleraine *171* arrived in resplendent blue. By all accounts her running had not been so good and now she had developed a hot 'big end'. Driver Joe Cairns started very briskly up to University and managed to knock two and a half

No 56 leaving Ballymoney with the 10.15 special from Antrim to Portrush on 8 April 1969.

Engine 171 arrives in Ballymoney with the 10.25 from York Road.

minutes off the branch schedule, without exceeding 39 mph. But Portrush was the end of her 'company' activities – she worked light back to Coleraine and was then stabled there until the next day when 5 came and rescued her, along with the stricken coaches.

One of the passengers on the 10.25 was a good schoolmate called John Bell. John had no particular interest in steam and compared to most conservative railway enthusiasts, he was a touch

No 53, with a rake of empty coaches, awaits the arrival of the 14.50 diesel from Belfast at Castlerock on 8 April.

Bohemian. He also liked to give the impression that he had 'something of a wild side'. His objective that day was to 'pick up a piece of talent'. So as John headed into Portrush town, the rest of us headed back to Coleraine in a dingy seven-car MED set (power units *8*, *18*, *19* and *20*). There we boarded an eight-car MPD set on the 11.45 York Road to Londonderry (cars *43*, *51*, *53*, *57* and *60*).

Derry, particularly that part of Derry which considers itself more Irish than British, is different from the rest of Northern Ireland in terms of celebrated holidays. In keeping with the Republic of Ireland, its citizens prefer to take Good Friday in lieu of Easter Tuesday. In summer the big holiday again coincides with the Republic's first Monday in August. So *53* had not been required for an excursion that morning, but she was needed to bring ten empty coaches back to Portrush to form an additional excursion to Belfast. We were all hoping that the magic that had worked on Saturday would do so again. It did and in fact we boarded the train in the yard – close to the place where the new Londonderry station lies.

Jeep *53* became the last one to ever stable at Londonderry overnight. She had not been turned – this would be done at Coleraine – therefore Bertie Davis and Albert Plews worked the big empty train bunk first (see page 12). Nothing more than 52 mph was attained before a stop at Castlerock. Not that this mattered; it was just nice to take in the best of Northern Ireland's railway scenery, such as the Magilligan strand at Downhill. Furthermore, coal was now starting to run low in the engine's bunker, so Bertie was making as efficient a run as possible. Switching engines at Coleraine preserved some more of *53*'s coal. While *53* was turned, *4*, with Jackie Kitchen driving, took us the last six miles into Portrush.

171's demise meant that for the second night running, number *10* was despatched from York Road. Also, there were still concerns about the lack of coal in *53*'s bunker. To remedy matters, *53* was rostered to the first excursion leaving at 18.40 – a light six-coach affair that would be easy on resources. Number *10* had come up light engine and had plenty of coal. So, for her last ever run out of Portrush, she was assigned to the non-stop 19.15, with the ten-coach load recently arrived from Derry. Number *4* was assigned to the 19.30, with the seven-coach load that had been *171*'s. Finally, *56* would make the anchor run at 19.45, with the nine coaches that had come up on the 09.25. All in all, Portrush had seen five engines that day – thereafter three would be the most the seaside town would ever boast.

John Bell turned up for the 18.40 and I decided to accompany him as far as Ballymoney. Enthusiast Mac Arnold's pre-run pep talk would eventually work wonders with driver Paddy Dobbin and fireman Albert Plews – but for that story you must refer to his book. Initially the run was competent – but no fireworks! Making 47 mph after the Portstewart slack was sprightly and we left Coleraine a few seconds ahead of schedule. We didn't quite touch 53 mph after Macfin – a little disappointing for a light train and I wondered if the coal problem was becoming acute. Meanwhile, John had spied a dark-haired girl on the opposite (non-milepost) side of the train. He drew my attention both to her and to his intentions. But since no-one could scale the heights of the pedestal upon which I'd placed the 'angel in blue', she just looked to me (and I'm sure I was utterly wrong) like any other girl! So I detrained at Ballymoney, wished John good luck and agreed to meet next term. This was a mistake. John got the girl (they went steady for a long time afterwards) and Mac Arnold got a great run once the coal reserves were deemed ample enough to oblige! The rest of us doubled back to Coleraine with the same MPD set that had been on the 11.45 (but minus power car *53*). At Coleraine, *10* ran through with the ten-coach non-stop 19.15. Despite the load, driver Bertie Wright ran through to Belfast without taking water – an unusual achievement for such a big train.

Fifteen minutes later Jackie Kitchen, aided and abetted by fireman Willie Graham, and number *4* arrived. This combination of men and machine would provide fun for the steam-loving masses for years to come, after official steam had ended. But tonight they had their hands full, as *4* had one steam injector failed and the second threatening to do the same. We started competently out of Coleraine, but were in trouble by Macfin. Then

The famous combination – driver Jackie Kitchen and fireman Willie Graham.

he got the second injector going again and we made Ballymoney only for it to fail again, right at the foot of Ballyboyland bank. So, no traction and down to 13 mph at Milepost 52, before life sprung back into the glass. This gave the band of assembled hooligans on the 19.30 (the Easter Tuesday run was renowned for bad or even immoral behaviour) a chance to play a game of jumping off and reboarding the train – somewhat different to some of the other activities they would get up to! The interlude was brief, however, as once Jackie got the injector going we accelerated quickly to 35 mph at Ballyboyland cabin, held 32 mph over Milepost 48 and managed 56 mph at Glarryford. The injector failure had cost us nearly seven minutes by Ballymena. In an attempt to pick up some time the tanks were only partially replenished and we were away for Belfast with what was one of my smartest ever starts out of Ballymena. Running at over 60 mph before Milepost 30, we should have been looking for a mid-60 maximum. Then the injector packed up again and so, after passing Kellswater in nicely under six minutes (at 62 mph), we drifted back to 47 mph at Milepost 26 and were down to 40 mph on the easy terrain before Antrim. Jackie tentatively got the device functioning again, which enabled us to accelerate to 48 mph at Dunadry, fall to 40 mph over Milepost 17 and then run the rest of the way up to Kingsbog at a satisfactory 42–43 mph. Once over the top you could almost sense the relief. Between gravity and brake applications we actually touched 60 mph at Whiteabbey – the final stop in Belfast was just outside the schedule of 41 minutes in from Ballymena – and just nine minutes late. A disappointing time for a relatively light load, but eventful none the less.

My only regret was that I had not waited at Ballymena for *56* on her final tribute to the main line. With the same nine-coach load as on Monday night, Ballymena driver Tom Smith had held a very impressive 45 mph over Kingsbog Junction. Nevertheless, it had been a wonderful Easter – one when three songs in particular had dominated the airwaves: 'The Israelites', 'I Heard it Through the Grapevine' and 'The Boxer'.

Tuesday 15 April

Another term – Easter now seemed a long time ago. This evening I found myself on the 17.10 train home. I can't recall what excuse I'd made to delay the homeward trip. Certainly the reason was not cross-country training, for oddly enough I had a competitive race to attend that evening. Neither do I record that the 'angel in blue' was on board the usual four-car BUT set (power units *124* and *131*). But there is one piece of evidence that makes it absolutely certain that she was present in the rear coach – my handwriting! It is so neat that it's almost copperplate. Now, I may have been no oil painting, but I was making sure that if this young woman had ever glanced over my shoulder to see the facts and figures that were being recorded, the neatness of the script would not have been found wanting – such foolish games!

Driver Tommy Carroll was not getting much pep out of the unit, so there was plenty of time between mileposts to ensure that figures were recorded neatly and accurately. Speed just exceeded 41 mph before Dunmurry, 45 mph before Hilden and 32 mph before Lisburn, on a dull but up to time run.

After a quick and not too indigestible tea, I was back on the 18.30 from Lisburn, courtesy of a three-car AEC-unit. Judging by the performance, one of the four engines in power cars *112* or *113* was out of action. In those days the 18.30 was the last Belfast-bound train to serve Balmoral and Adelaide halts. After 7.00 pm, local trains ran non-stop to and from Finaghy. My race was actually at Balmoral, so I was able to detrain there. That there should have been an evening race along the leafy glades of Harberton Park, was entirely due to an outbreak of 'foot and mouth' disease during the previous November. The Malcolm Cup was usually (for under 18s) a three-mile cross-country race run over Barnett's Park, that took place on the last Saturday in November. For health and safety reasons it had to be postponed and was eventually run as a road race on this particular evening. I recall running reasonably well, finishing about twentieth in a field of a hundred or so. Afterwards, I had to make my way back to Finaghy station, where a three-car BUT set (cars *125* and *127*) on the 20.45 ex-Great Victoria Street was also experiencing problems with engine failures.

However, there was an advantage in having multi-engined stock. Even as the likelihood of engine failures increased, most trains got by on three out of four or four out of six working. Maybe NIR should take note (if it ever gets the green light to restock), as the problem it has faced over recent years has been largely caused by having ageing three-car units powered by one engine only. When that fails, you sit and watch the countryside!

Friday 25 April

At the time of writing there is still a train that leaves Great Victoria Street at 17.21 each weekday evening and serves Central at 17.30 and Yorkgate at 17.35. This train is all that is left of the 17.30 business express to Larne Harbour (serving Carrickfergus, Whitehead, Ballycarry and Larne Town). But it incorporates the ghosts of lots of other local trains as well and stops everywhere. It is usually operated by a five- or six-car '80-class' unit. When NIR eventually decide to replace these units, it would be appropriate if this was the last turn to go, since, in 1969, the 17.30 was the last scheduled passenger train in Ireland to be regularly steam-hauled.

It was commonplace for a crowd of enthusiasts to assemble at York Road on a Friday evening – on other evenings there might just have been one or two. So far, April had been a rather barren month for steam on the 17.30 – I have not described all the days that we stood watching until a diesel appeared in platform two. This particular evening we were all fairly relaxed about things, for it was the weekend of the Brian Boru Railtour to Cork, featuring *4* and *171*. Whatever happened, we were all guaranteed a feast of steam – even if it was in preservation mode. Of course, you always get a feast or a famine and so, to complete the feast tonight, the 17.30 was steam-hauled.

The engine involved was number *6*. Once a revered member of her class, she had been one of the last to gain a full overhaul in 1965. Whatever was done to her then, she never returned to her previous form. Even the number on her front buffer beam was a cheap two-dimensional transfer, instead of the nicely painted '3-D effect' numbers that were painted on the buffer beams of most other engines. It seemed to symbolise her fate. Notwithstanding, Paddy Shannon produced a reasonable effort with her and the standard six-coach load. He touched 49 mph at Whitehouse, held 40 mph over Whiteabbey and again at Greenisland and eased through Trooperslane at 52 mph. Then it was on to Whitehead and we managed 56 mph before the reverse curves at Milepost 13. This was a solid effort keeping time all the way.

The rest of the weekend would be fairly expensive, and to conserve cash I only went as far as Whitehead. The return working (the 19.15 ex-Larne Harbour) did some solid work too, with 55 mph exceeded at Downshire Park and a very satisfactory time of 7 m 24 s between Whitehead and Carrickfergus. Climbing the hill to Greenisland, *6* showed a bit of weakness, with just over 37 mph after Trooperslane. Thereafter much of the run was spoilt with signal checks – the 17.40 ex-Londonderry was due in just ahead of us, and if it was doing badly it could lead to hold-ups on the Larne side of Bleach Green Junction. The final run along the lough shore just netted 52 mph and an arrival at York Road just four minutes late, thanks to the 'Derry'.

Saturday 26 April

This is not a book about preservation. Neither would I wish to assume the role as a recorder of RPSI runs, which I know is a subject well catered for. Therefore, I will say nothing about the 'Brian Boru' Railtour, other than to record that it was enjoyable, at times exhilarating and never without incident! However, it was tinged with one little regret that I must record.

While we were all well south of Dublin, NIR submitted to a request by the Warwickshire Locomotive Society to have the 14.05 boat train steam-hauled. With the loss of steam in England, from 10 August 1968, more and more enthusiasts were making the journey across the Irish Sea to sample the delights of main line steam, that were still to be had in Northern Ireland. They would have felt quite at home, for the engines were unashamedly of an English (LMS) design, having been built at Derby between 1946 and 1950. The engine selected that day was *56* and this turned out to be the last passenger run she ever made. Looking back, I think I would have forgone the railtour, just to have experienced the last hurrah of *56*.

May 69

Sunday 4 May

My good friend Robert White, who lived in Holywood, came to visit today. He brought with him sad news. The previous week, *56* had smashed a cylinder head while on a spoil train at Magheramorne. She was never used again, but even her demise has a story. In 1966 she had been involved in a shameful mission – that of providing traction for the lifting train on the closed Portadown to Londonderry line. At Pomeroy, on 17 July, she went out of control and sustained damage to her front left cylinder head. She lay out of service until Adelaide shed was closed in November of that year. She was then hauled (by *51*) to York Road, where she was eventually repaired and re-entered service in time for the Apprentice Boys specials in August 1967. However, it appears that there was still some metal fatigue and so, on 29 April 1969, she finally succumbed.

Wednesday 7 May

"Have you heard the latest from Fleetwood Mac?" John Bell asked me one morning at breaktime. I hadn't, but I resolved to listen out for it. Back in '69 we weren't talking about the smooth US/UK five-piece that gave us the mega-selling 'Rumours' and 'Tango in the Night' albums. We meant the 'bluesy' Fleetwood Mac who had scored a number one with the unlikely instrumental 'Albatross', on the even less likely Blue Horizon label. " 'Man of the World' is even better" John enthused. Maybe it was the trip home on the 17.10, watching the 'angel in blue' out of the corner of my eye; maybe it was the disc jockey who obliged by playing the record later, when I'd set up my reel to reel tape recorder, with the microphone placed up against the speaker of an old valve radio; but for once a friend's glowing recommendation hardly did justice. I must have rewound and replayed the tape 20 times that evening and this plaintive song would quickly become my top desert island disc.

Friday 9 May

Once again the Friday ensemble of enthusiasts was not disappointed. Steam was required on the 17.30 to Larne Harbour. Number *4*, driven by Percy Mitchell, had a light five-coach load for the turn. The run both ways was competent enough, but not quite up to Percy's best, possibly because he was using the occasion to give his fireman a spot of driving experience! Nevertheless, 56 mph before Downshire Park on the way home is more than one could hope from today's DEMUs, with the single-line working that now exists between Whitehead and Kilroot.

It is strange to note, but here we were in 1969, the year after British Rail ceased all steam-hauled services (other than the Vale of Rheidol narrow gauge in Wales) and frequency of steam on this train was substantially up on 1968! There were several reasons for this, but the principal one concerned a contract, won in 1966, to transport many millions of tons of 'spoil' from a site close to the Magheramorne cement works to Greencastle, on the Lough shore. It is difficult to remember that in those days the M2 started at Greencastle and that there was no M5 or M2 approach road to Belfast City. The railway ran right along side the proposed route, which amounted to reclaiming land that had formerly belonged to Belfast Lough! The millions of tons

Stone Trains I: Nos 53 and 10 with a laden train at Whiteabbey on 5 April 1969.

Stone Trains II: Nos 51 and 56 on an 'up' train at Greencastle the same day.

of spoil would achieve this and would form the corridor upon which, today, the five-lane M2/M5 runs. Some commentators cynically mused that the railway was being made to dig its own grave, but I don't think that was fair comment. The last major closure of any line in Northern Ireland, the Portadown to Londonderry line, had taken place in 1965, and since then the route mileage has been remarkably static – indeed, the opening of the cross-harbour link in 1994 and the spur to Great Victoria Street in 1995 actually increased it slightly. Moreover, there was no motive power available for these spoil trains other than the few remaining 'jeeps', as they were affectionately known. These engines were still comparatively new by steam standards, having been built between 1946 and 1950 and, although no major 'shoppings' were done by York Road shed after 1966, minor overhauls still occurred.

Most passenger workings in the late 1960s

Stone trains III: Nos 53 and 51 on the 11.45 ex-Magheramorne approaching Whitehead on 28 February 1970.

were by diesel multiple units. The Great Northern section probably had the oldest stock and the potential for problems was exacerbated by paucity of spare parts. It operated ten AEC (of Great Western design) railcars, of 1950 vintage,and 14 BUTs dating from 1954 to 1958. The slightly more powerful BUTs had for some years been the regular stock for the Belfast-based 'Enterprise Express' to Dublin. There were four such trains per day, with CIÉ operating two by diesel electric locomotive and coaches. The six-car BUT set rostered for this turn would leave Belfast at 08.00 and 14.30, returning from Dublin at 11.00 and 17.30. The staff at Grosvenor Road shed worked tirelessly to ensure that the set turned out was in tip-top condition. If cars were dubious, and thought to be prime suspects for engine failures, they would be placed on less important turns. Until a year ago this had worked well, but then even the 'crack train' started to suffer delays and breakdowns due to mechanical failures. Since 1966, NIR had been operating the York Road to Londonderry services with the new 'Hampshire' diesel electric multiple units (DEMUs). However, a policy change resulted in the sending of a six-car Hampshire set to the GN

section to take over the Dublin services (see page 97). Railcar numbers on both GN and NCC sections were to be balanced by the interchange of a six-car AEC set to York Road. And so it was that on the evening of Sunday 5 January 1969 (the end of a very bad weekend in what was to become the thirty years of Northern Ireland's 'troubles') a five-car AEC set, comprising power cars *117*, *118* and *120*, trundled through Lisburn, en route for Antrim and thence to York Road. Sister *119* (nicknamed 'the foghorn' because of a less than efficient silencer on one of her engines) missed the party, for she was currently being shopped, but the intention was for her to follow later.

Two things then happened that would change the pattern of steam on the evening business express to Larne for the next eight months. Firstly, the six-car Hampshire set could not seat as many passengers as a six-car BUT set. This was because nearly half of the front and rear power units housed the diesel-electric engine. The old DMUs had their engines (two per powered car) conveniently placed under the passenger carrying compartment. So NIR had to respond by sending a further two-car unit, making three Hampshire power units in all at work on the GN. Secondly, the York Road men had severe trouble getting to grips with the more antiquated AEC gearboxes, compared to their newer multi-purpose diesels (MPDs). A five-car AEC unit could be a little shy on power at the best of times, but gear failures would make them unworkable. The inevitable happened on 9 January at Larne Harbour, with the 15.00 train to York Road. When the AECs were hauled by a steam engine back to York Road, that evening the 17.30 was steam for the first time in many months. It was not long before the AEC set (see page 9) was sent back to Great Victoria Street and York Road had to count the cost of a net loss of three Hampshire units. That was sufficient to change the presence of steam on the 17.30 from a rare event to, at times, an almost daily occurrence. I was determined to make the most of it, for such would never come my way again!

Saturday 10 May

After an early start from Lisburn, it was across to York Road on foot. There was just one steam hauled 'Sunday School' excursion to Portrush, and tickets had to be obtained from the convener. Would he sell me a ticket? Could I become an honorary member of yet another Sunday School – for just a day? I always dressed fairly conservatively for these occasions and tried not to pose a threat. He sold me a ticket. It was a wet morning and I curled up in a not particularly warm seat. The woman opposite was homely and smiled at me, and I recalled that quiet sophistication and serenity of women in maturity that so characterised the 'angel in blue'. We were late getting away, while York Road shed sorted out operations. The train, a nine-coach load, would not usually be entitled to a pilot engine to Kingsbog Junction. But NIR, in satisfying a request from the then relatively recently formed Railway Preservation Society of Ireland, to have the 14.05 Larne boat train steam-hauled for people attending their open day at Whitehead, had a spare engine (see page 45). Number 5 (always a difficult engine to get a run with) had been selected for this and, presumably as a warm up, was also tasked with piloting 4 to Kingsbog. In fact, this was the second time in just three weeks that NIR had kindly satisfied a request by enthusiasts to have the train substituted by steam.

Larne Harbour: 5 awaits departure of the 17.15 to York Road on 10 May 1969.

The RPSI open day's attraction for mainstream enthusiasts also meant that I found myself their only representative on the alternate steam turn. Bertie Wright was charged with *4*, while Jackie Kitchen was having a bit of fun on *5*'s footplate. The right away, when it eventually came, was worth waiting for. The two engines took the nine coaches away to 55 mph before Whitehouse, then never fell below 37 mph on the 1/75 bank to Ballyclare Junction, eventually stopping at Kingsbog in just 14 m 47 s after leaving York Road. This run claims a place in my top three climbs of Mossley bank. Sadly, we had to say goodbye to *5* and her crew, but Wright and *4* were commendable the rest of the way to Portrush. Had it not been for a signal check just before Ballymena, the 22 and a bit miles from Kingsbog would have been covered in 25 minutes, with 67 mph at Dunadry, 64 mph again after Antrim, momentarily below 53 mph up to Post 26 and then 61 mph at Kellswater. Fifteen miles at 'even time' (i.e. an average of 60 mph or better) was a daily event in steam express days – but it wasn't always the case with a heavily laden and easily timed excursion. The single line section on to Portrush was competently handled, once number *4* recovered from a heavy bout of slipping on the incline out of Ballymena. Wright managed 56 mph before Dunloy, exceeded 65 mph down Ballyboyland and touched 58 mph at Macfin, before the A26 road-bridge strengthening slack put paid to any chance of a big speed down 'the housing estate' before Coleraine. Arrival at Portrush, at five past eleven, was close to time. The weather, which had caused the slipping at Ballymena, was at last starting to improve. I was grateful for this, for with no other enthusiasts around, a long and rather solitary day lay ahead.

However, such days are good for reflection and I'd been doing plenty of that recently. Furthermore, I had something else to concentrate my mind on that afternoon. Although this was my year between O' and A' levels, I had elected to take double maths as two A' level subjects. The procedure at Methodist College was to enter such candidates in the single subject at the end of the lower sixth year. If a candidate attained a grade A, then only further maths was taken at the end of the second year, otherwise you were given another chance at single maths. I was hoping to do well enough to avoid the repeat, so, for a while, I crept into an empty coach compartment and got some work done.

While the coaches from the excursion train stayed at Portrush, the engine did not. As soon as the train had been shunted and a path to Coleraine became available, Wright and *4* would be away, and would not return until maybe half an hour before the scheduled departure home. At Coleraine, the engine would be turned, the fire partially dropped and, for the afternoon, *4* would be permitted to simmer like a sleepy old dog in the spring sunshine, beyond the engine shed. Had it been the previous year, the entire Portrush branch would have gone silent, awaiting the engine's return, for since 1960 the branch only operated normal passenger services in the summer period, between mid June and early September. But the opening of the New University at Coleraine in September 1968 had changed all that. With the close proximity of the railway to the new campus and the prospect of students with 'digs' in Coleraine or Portrush, NIR had, for once, seized an opportunity and had constructed a short platform simply called 'University', where trains called on request. They had also reverted to providing a year-long service on the branch, seven days a week. So, on this day there would have been arrivals and departures of the branch diesel, at roughly hourly intervals.

Engine and driver returned in good time, well prepared to make the scheduled departure at 19.15. Now different drivers would adopt different styles of running, in order to keep to schedule. Bertie Wright had become the master of the economical run home. Basically the plan was as follows: work the engine hard up the hills, run very easily and economically elsewhere and conserve enough water to avoid a stop at Ballymena, thereby gaining about five minutes. This run home was a model of his plan.

We made an excellent start up the 1/76 out of Portrush, with 31 mph attained at Post 66 and 47 mph (the overall speed limit on the Portrush branch was 40 mph) before passing Coleraine in under 12 m 30 s. Then the bridge slack took its toll, with no more than 48 mph before Ballymoney, where a very slow tablet exchange was made. That slack seemed to inspire the driver for he 'hammered' 4 up Ballyboyland bank with 39 mph at the cabin and a minimum of 37 mph thereafter and stopped in Dunloy in plenty of time to await the arrival of the 19.00 MPD set from York Road. Nothing more than 52 mph was attained at Glarryford and Dunminning and, as expected, 4 had sufficient water on board to avoid the Ballymena stop. More economical work on the double line ensued with 57 mph attained at Kellswater, 49 mph at Post 26 and 55 mph before Antrim. On the uphill section to Kingsbog Junction 4 was again worked harder, with speed momentarily falling below 40 mph at Post 17 (and again at Post 12), but recovering to 45 mph through Templepatrick. Even a trundle down Mossley bank and signal checks along the lough shore, could not prevent Wright being only a few minutes late into the terminus.

Friday 16 May

Steam men were not supposed to like DMUs, and in general I didn't. However, I had a soft spot for the ex-GNR AECs, introduced back in 1950 and now fairly long in the tooth! They were so obviously of an elegant Great Western Railway design (having been built at Park Royal in north-west London) and had high-backed comfortable seats, particularly in the first class compartment, which was now open to second class passengers, since first class travel had been abolished on all commuter trains. Ten of these units went into UTA and later NIR ownership, and were numbered 111–120. The odd numbered cars faced Dublin – the even numbers faced Belfast, and usually a set comprised three coaches, an even numbered power unit, an odd numbered power unit and an intermediate trailer. Routinely, I collected a lot of data on them – an analysis of

their performance on non-stop Belfast to Lisburn trains, disproved the theory that they were all equal in terms of power. In particular, units 117, 119, 116, 114 and 112 were more powerful than the other five. On this particular day, four of the better units formed two three-car sets and the results illustrate the case. The 16.15 ex-Great Victoria Street had units 112 and 117 in three-car formation and achieved 59 mph before Lisburn. (I never recorded more than 60 mph with this type of DMU and 54 mph would have been average.) More notably, Charlie Mulgrave had a three-car set, comprising units 116 and 119, on the 17.45 local to Lisburn. This train then returned empty to Belfast. I was permitted to join him for the return journey, and speeds of 58 mph at Derriaghy and 72 mph at Post 110, before shutting off power, were exceptional. Had Charlie kept power on to Adelaide, my 75 mph record might just have fallen. Bobby Quail had achieved this two years previously, with 117 and 118 on a three-car set, but even this driver could not better his own steam record, where jeep 55 exceeded 76 mph through Adelaide, laden with an eight-coach special returning from Dublin on 14 July 1966.

Saturday 17 May

Another day of Sunday School excursions. This week there were two trains rostered, though the second ran empty to Ballymena and picked up children, teachers and friends there. Robert White accompanied me for the trip, but otherwise there was still a surprising paucity of enthusiasts. The previous week, Bertie Wright (who was a good driver up a hill!) had been given a pilot to Kingsbog. This week the first excursion was in the hands of Harry Ramsey, a great friend and engineman, but if a train was easily timed, as many of these excursions were, then he might be spared having to work the engine particularly hard. York Road shed have given him 53, a ten-coach load, a Whiteabbey stop just at the foot of the 1/75 climb to Ballyclare Junction and no sign of any pilot!

First, Robert and I had to secure tickets, for, like the previous week, this was an all Sunday

School charter train. We eventually did so, from the superintendent of one of the local churches and, although the price was slightly more than the standard day return fare to Portrush, we were pleased to note that the tickets included lunch at a local church hall! So, freed from the prospect of greasy sausage, egg and chips in a seaside cafe, and with the sun peeping out from behind a cloud, we were looking forward to the day out with great optimism.

Harry (and *53*) was in no hurry out to Whiteabbey, taking nearly 11 minutes and barely exceeding 35 mph, establishing the dubious record of my worst run out the lough shore! Here, the local Presbyterian church was also looking forward to a pleasant outing, and four minutes was spent loading passengers and crates of lemonade. It was quite clear that *53* was giving no trouble whatsoever, as a sure footed climb to Mossley at 15–16 mph was made and by Ballyclare Junction the speed had risen to 23 mph. At Mossley, we looked back down the hill and could see *4*, with her empty excursion train, halted at Bleach Green viaduct, still awaiting *53's* progress! Harry just about touched 64 mph at Dunadry, with 56 mph into the dip after Antrim, but lack of working the engine allowed speed to fall to a miserable 37 mph at Post 26, before achieving 53 mph at Kellswater. Another sure-footed, but lazy, climb out of Ballymena followed, with 50 mph attained just before Dunloy, where the most notable thing of the day was the hand tablet exchange taken at a rather excessive (and quite sore on the arm) 47 mph! Harry just touched 60 mph down Ballyboyland and 50 mph at Macfin, before the bridge slack. This type of running would generally be described as extremely dull, yet Robert and I were enjoying every minute of it. It was just one of those 'good to be alive' days.

At Portrush we didn't take time to pay our regards to Harry – we would do so later – as it was off to Dhu Varren for a photograph of *4* on the next steam special. Dhu Varren halt was also conveniently situated near the church hall where lunch was to be served. This consisted of lots of sandwiches and copious buns and we had tea, out of one of those enormous two-handled steel teapots, served by a pretty dark-haired girl who looked both familiar and quizzical.

Imagine the scene – a lovely May evening in Portrush station thirty years ago. Engine 53 has her ten coaches at Platform 2 and they are already staring to fill up. Only a few people have yet boarded *4's* train at Platform 3, which will leave a little later. More lemonade is being loaded into a guard's compartment of the busier train. Now, I was never terribly dextrous – I was hopeless at ball sports and if it hadn't been for some God-given motor power, which gave me some ability at running and cycling, I would have been a complete waste of time to the school from a sporting point of view. So much more then the achievement for me, to catch, in one hand, a crate of lemonade as it headed quickly back in the general direction of the platform, having been loaded without due concern for its centre of gravity! The thought that some children (and indeed some grown-ups) would not be denied their refreshment, as *53* headed for home, simply added to the bonhomie of the occasion.

Engine *53* got the right away a few minutes late and made a lazy climb up past Dhu Varren. As usual, once over the top of the hill, Harry barely altered *53's* settings; consequently a tolerable 45 mph was attained before a bad signal check at Coleraine, the A26 bridge slack, and further non-expansive running meant that little more was done before Ballymoney.

Up Ballyboyland bank, Harry allowed *53* to fall below 24 mph at Posts 52 and 49, despite a reasonable recovery in between. I was a little bemused, though. My first ever run on a return Sunday School excursion had been three years previously. On that occasion Harry had been in charge of number *6*, with a load of nine coaches, and progress at this point had been identical. There was plenty of time to look out of the coach and see Harry's hatted silhouette casting long shadows in the evening sunshine, as *53's* long, lazy, slowing exhaust headed towards the reverse curves at Post 49. I like to think that, like me, he was just savouring this timeless scene so much that he didn't want it to be over too quickly! Alternatively, he could have been just wasting time so that the tardy diesel would have to make the crossing stop at Dunloy, and he would get clean through. More time was wasted down to Post 47, ensuring that this was precisely what happened.

After Dunloy, *53* was opened up a little and 54 mph was achieved round the Dunminning curves. With a ten-coach load, there was little chance of the water stop at Ballymena being omitted, though, with less than two and a half minutes spent doing this, I guess the tanks were only partially topped up. A speed of 55 mph at Kellswater was hardly a record, but it was the best of the run home. Speed then fell to 47 mph at Post 26 and any chance of a run through Antrim was lost due to a signal check at Post 24. (Harry would usually attempt to get a heavy train away in excess of 60 mph at Antrim to give him a reasonable start up the 11 mile bank to Kingsbog Junction.) So it was 45 mph through Antrim instead of the desired mile-a-minute. Strangely, that seemed to inspire Harry and for the first time that day we actually heard *53* being worked hard. Consequently, the 330-ton train had recovered to 51 mph at Muckamore and speed held above 40 mph until a mile short of the summit, with a final minimum of 39 mph at Kingsbog. Holding 40 mph all the way to the summit, with a ten-coach train, was always regarded as solid work. Thereafter we trundled down the hill (55 mph maximum), stopped at Whiteabbey for five minutes and ran competently along the shore and into the terminus.

A trio of songs played that day, all of them by then relatively uncharted Motown artists. Indeed, they form, in sequence, the last three tracks of the 'Motown Chartbusters Volume 3' compilation, and if this book could only have one choice of album to create the musical mood of the era then, I guess, this would have to be it. The songs were 'Behind A Painted Smile' (Isley Brothers); 'Road Runner' (Junior Walker and the All Stars); and 'The Tracks of My Tears' (Smokey Robinson and the Miracles). Now, see if you can better that for quality!

Monday 19 May

This morning, a dark-haired girl stopped me in the corridor and asked "Do you not recognise me, and did you enjoy your day out on Saturday?" What questions! Didn't she know I was living every minute as if dear life itself depended on it! But she was friendly. It was a pity she was in the middle sixth (the year above me – who were sitting their full A' levels), for she and most of her compatriots would, within a week or so, depart on study leave. Apart from examination days, that would be the end of their involvement with Methody. Mind you, it crossed my mind more than once that I would be better fitted amorously pursuing the possible, instead of unattainable glamourous icons on the homebound train! (Unfortunately, Cupid's arrows had struck before I'd realised that the 'angel in blue' was very married.) In the meantime, the heart ruled the head, and although good sense would ultimately prevail, it would take just a little more time in coming!

Friday 23 May

Almost as if to prove the fine fettle of *53*, she turned up on the 17.30 in the hands of the driver Alan Robinson and young fireman Arthur McMenamin. Fellow enthusiast and schoolmate Alex Lindsay confirmed that the driver had produced some marvellous runs that week, for on Wednesday evening he had had number *5* into Carrickfergus in under 13½ minutes. Number *53* was generally regarded as a stronger engine. We were over a minute late away, with a relatively light load of five coaches. A fast start to Seaview was followed by an unusually cautious run along the lough shore (nothing more than 47 mph). By Whiteabbey speed was down to 41 mph, but Al recovered to 47 mph by Jordanstown and held this all the way up to Greenisland. An easy run down the 'Mount' still attained 60 mph and a very creditable 14 minute time to Carrickfergus. Thereafter, this run simply improved – to the extent that there were several sections well beyond the capabilities of today's 80-class and 450-class units. The section on to Whitehead produced 58 mph and a seven-minute timing (despite catching an adverse distant signal coming into Whitehead) and ensured that departure from here was spot on time. The difficult section to Ballycarry was settled in less than four minutes and a maximum of 44 mph. The final section to Larne Town (then situated where the back of Murrayfield shopping centre is today) was the best I ever recorded – 55 mph – before a hand tablet exchange at Magheramorne loop (taken at a leisurely 28 mph). Then Al was away to 61 mph through 'the Glynn', before stopping in Larne absolutely on time (not a regular event for this train) in nine minutes and 44 seconds.

The run home, with the load now reduced to four coaches, was fabulous too. A maximum speed of 38 mph before a stop at Glynn was competent work, while 49 mph before Magheramorne was excellent! The hand tablet at Magheramorne loop was again taken in leisurely fashion, before racing away to 55 mph and the Ballycarry stop. Up the hill to Whitehead, Al produced no less than 45 mph and an unbelievable start to stop time of three minutes and 35 seconds. The run to Carrickfergus was excellent too, with 64 mph at Kilroot and a start to stop time of six minutes and 29 seconds (allowed eight minutes!). Until then I'd never had an under five minute time from Carrickfergus to Greenisland, but that record fell too with speeds of 39 mph at 'the Mount' and almost 49 mph after Trooperslane and a stopping time in Greenisland of four minutes and 58 seconds. Down to Jordanstown the speed just exceeded 46 mph, with a start to stop time of two minutes and 36 seconds. So good was this run that the inevitable happened – the 17.40 MPD ex-Derry was running a few minutes late and we were stopped by signals before joining the main line. That cost us nearly three minutes, but 53 made up most of the lost time by running in from Whiteabbey in six minutes and 40 seconds, with a maximum of 60 mph along the shore. Experiencing days like these, we could be forgiven for thinking that the end of steam was light years away!

Saturday 24 May

Friday's optimism soon evaporated. This Saturday, Sunday School excursionists had to vie for space with a different set of tourists, for this was the day of the annual Northwest 200 motorcycle races at Portrush. As such, a more unruly element on board was a distinct possibility. York Road shed produced *51* and a ten-coach load for the first excursion of the day, due to leave at 09.05. This engine, generally renowned for being a strong engine with a heavy load up a hill, but never one to thrill with big speeds, had not been on the main line for nearly a year and had worked very few passenger trains of any description since the previous summer. A Ballymena man, and by reputation a good engineman, Tom Smith was in charge. Right from the off (just one minute late) we were in trouble. Before we even reached Seaview, it appeared that somebody in the second coach had tried, unsuccessfully, to pull the communication chord (not behaviour associated with a Sunday School excursion!) I say unsuccessfully, for the train was not halted, but there is a chance that a dragging brake had a hand in the events which followed. Tom struggled with *51* to attain 40 mph along the shore, but as soon as he hit the adverse gradient to Whiteabbey and Mossley, speed fell faster than leaves on a stormy autumn day. We were just crossing Bleach Green viaduct when fellow timer Joe Cassells appeared down the train, eyes intently serious, with the observation that we weren't going to make it (i.e. *51* would stall on the 1/75 gradient). None of us wanted that. Notwithstanding the fact that diesels failed and were rescued by steam engines all the time, if the authorities heard of a steam failure, it would be taken as another good reason to hasten the day of their total demise. By Monkstown, the speed was down to six mph and our fate looked sealed. But Tom fought and fought with *51*, as black 'stour' and smoke wafted down the train. Some revellers jumped out on to the line-side, showed that they could run along the bank faster than the train and then prised their way back on through an illegally opened door. (Again this was not behaviour to be expected from Sunday School excursionists.) By Mossley the speed had fallen below five mph, but we were at least still moving, and Tom had just got *51* over the worst part of the bank. From there a gradual recovery set in, but over 41 minutes had elapsed since leaving York Road by the time we stopped at Kingsbog Junction, apparently as a result of another cord pull. Away from Kingsbog, *51* was worked so easily down the hill that it was after Antrim before 50 mph was exceeded. Surprisingly then, we only fell momentarily below 45 mph at Post 26, showing that the engine had some capability of being worked, but only 52 mph was attained at Kellswater. I had other runs with Tom Smith and one consistent feature of these was that although he would run hard up a hill, he seldom exceeded 50 mph.

A large tribe of enthusiasts understandably detrained at Ballymena and watched *51* starting away quite briskly out of the station, up the cutting towards Cullybackey. Then the dirty black 'stour' reappeared from *51*'s chimney and we never did get to know whether it was the partially pulled communication chord, or bad coal, or a dirty smokebox, or some other combination of problems that had caused the trouble.

Naturally, when one train gets into trouble, nothing seems to run particularly well. The delay to *51* meant that everything behind and everything in both directions on the single line to Portrush was affected. (In those days the railway was double track from York Road to Ballymena.) Hence, Bertie Wright was over half an hour late out of Ballymena with *4* and a ten-coach special. The usual hand tablet slacks were augmented by a series of signal checks at Cullybackey, before stopping at Coleraine, as well as a permanent way slack at Glarryford. Consequently the speed was no more than 50 mph before Dunloy, 58 mph down Ballyboyland and 55 mph before Macfin. The best of the work was to better the 15-minute allowance along the Portrush branch by nearly three minutes, without exceeding the branch limit of 40 mph!

We stuck with Wright and *4* for the run home, one which he intended to craft in a similar vein to that of two weeks previous. However, the extra coach or problems with steaming meant that, at first, it was generally inferior. True, we exceeded 47 mph on the branch, but then had an extra stop at Ballymoney. So, from a standing start 34 mph was attained at Ballyboyland cabin and 31 mph was held over the top. Once the diesel, running late as usual, had been crossed at Dunloy, running seemed to pick up a little. We reached 55 mph around Dunminning, before a stop at Ballymena. On the double line 56 mph was reached at Kellswater and 58 mph after Cookstown Junction. This night we also had an Antrim stop. Wright was making plenty of noise starting up the cutting towards Muckamore and had notched *4* and her 330-ton load up to 44 mph by Post 19. But then, as so often could be the case for a heavy train starting out of Antrim, *4* got slightly winded on the steepest part of the bank, at Dunadry, and speed fell back towards 35 mph. That seemed to give the driver much needed incentive, for Wright started putting *4* through her paces and recovered to 43 mph just after Templepatrick. We would have gone over the top at 42 mph had he not caught sight of an adverse distant signal at Kingsbog. Even so, he still held over 40 mph and down the hill almost touched the illusive 60 mph at Mossley, before a somewhat tentative stop to position the long train at Whiteabbey, reached in a creditable 23 minutes from Antrim. The final stretch along the lough shore was competently handled with 50 mph exceeded and thoughts of even better days to come!

Sunday 25 May

Sunday was not a day when one could expect any steam passenger workings, but for the past year there had been steam-hauled ballast workings on the former Great Northern section on Tuesdays, Thursdays and Sundays. This involved a light engine travelling from York Road to Antrim, thence to Lisburn on the branch which had been used only for goods' trains, stock movements and the occasional excursion train since 1960, and on to Great Victoria Street to pick up the ballast wagons. So the engine and crew would clock up 47 miles each way just to get into

No 10 at Lisburn on 25 May 1969 with new 'Hampshire' units on a local train.

position! Today this would be a simple three-mile run through Central, Botanic and City Hospital, but back then this was only a pipe dream! For most of the first year of these workings the mainstay engine was number *3*. She had been damaged, apparently beyond repair, in the previous March and *5* had become the regular 'ballast' engine. However, with no spoil trains on Sundays, York Road shed had more freedom of choice as to which engine would be sent. So, shortly after 'Crusaders' (a Christian outreach organisation working with teenagers, mainly from a grammar school background, attended without fail between 3.00 and 4.00 pm in the little hall in Graham Gardens, which is now home to the Lisburn Fellowship Church), I got on my bike and cycled to Brookmount and Brookhill. There I was rewarded with a very summery photograph of *10* returning to York Road. She would be back on Great Northern metals in a very different role before the week was over.

Monday 26 May

This was a bank (and school) holiday. NIR took the opportunity to get some track repairs done. So two engines (*5* and *6*) were involved on ballast trains on the GN section, and I noted them returning to York Road together with the GN directors' saloon in the following order: *5* chimney-first, directors' saloon and *6* bunk-first. Now if that formation had been fully developed, it could have cast anything possible by even a 2x2-car 80-class into insignificance!

Tuesday 27 May

My good friends, the NIR station staff at Lisburn, provided me with some very interesting information. Apparently a consortium of churches and clubs in the Portadown area had asked to charter a special train to Portrush next Saturday and NIR had agreed to their request. Indeed, rumour was rife that there would be two steam specials from Portadown to Portrush. The last through Portadown to Portrush specials had been in 1966 – before Adelaide shed had closed. Since then, the logistics had been deemed too awkward and such trade had been shunned. Perhaps now, the 'ballast' train served as a reminder of what was possible.

Wednesday 28 May

Number *53* was an unusual choice for the ballast train today. However, she brought with her the directors' saloon, and this vehicle then appears to have been attached to the ballast train for the purpose of the annual track inspection. Since all NIR metals have to be inspected, permission had being granted for the train to advance to Dundalk, where the engine would run round the train for the return journey. This was probably the only time a steam engine on company business (as opposed to RPSI outings) ventured there after the closure of Adelaide shed. The higher than usual route mileage and the fact that *53*, unlike usual choices for ballast, was equipped with the larger coal capacity 'high bunk' was probably the reason for her appearance.

Thursday 29 May

This was a Thursday more like those earlier in the year, when after school cross-country training would, of necessity, dictate a late train home. Mind you, there were numerous occasions when I could have easily made the fast 16.50 or even the slow 16.55 – but purposely didn't! So now, within the time frame which can loosely be called 'the summer', I can describe a typical run on the 17.10. As with that eventful afternoon in January, a four-car BUT set formed the train. Already people were beginning to start and end their working day in Belfast somewhat earlier, so traffic on this train was gradually increasing, while that on later trains fell. Indeed, before the end of the year this train would be the subject of a letter in the *Belfast Telegraph*, where the miserly four-car arrangement would be likened to a cattle truck! However, this evening both the 'angel in blue' and myself were seated comfortably – at the scene of the crime in car *121*! Number *134* supplied power at the front and we were just under two minutes late away from Great Victoria Street. A seven and a half minute run before the first stop at Dunmurry (maximum 42 mph) was slightly below average, but underscored the slightly underpowered nature of this car formation. Four and three quarter minutes on to Hilden, just exceeding 45 mph at Lambeg, followed by the customary two and a half minutes to Lisburn, meant no time had been gained. But then, it could have taken half a lifetime and I wouldn't have cared!

Friday 30 May

The 'angel in blue' also shared my regular morning inbound train, though somehow romance and that feeling of danger and illicitness were mainly confined to the homeward 17.10. Maybe that was because in the choice of morning train I had little freedom, but schoolboys (and girls!) should be away home soon after four, so to turn up on the 17.10 so regularly seemed almost like an invasion of her privacy! Anyway, this morning, while waiting for the 08.12 (all stops except Derriaghy), we were entertained by the appearance of *53* running light to Great Victoria Street. Again the high bunk was needed, as *53* had more than ballast duties ahead of her.

Leaving for home on the 16.15 (if any could warrant the description then this was my regular train home), I noted *53* already back from her ballast duties and preparing a set of seven coaches. So it was a very quick change at home and back to the terminus within the hour, for *53* was obviously going to position the coaches at Portadown for tomorrow's excursion. The rush-hour traffic was allowed to clear and therefore I still had time to find a friendly guard and ask if I could travel on the empty coaches. An affirmative was received and my evening was made.

The driver rostered was none other than Bobby Quail, previously mentioned herein for heroics with engine *55* and who, years later, would be the architect of some excellent runs on the 'Steam Enterprise'. Preservation would come soon enough, but tonight Portadown would receive coaches for its last ever steam-hauled train in 'NIR' days.

We edged out behind the 18.35 fast train to Portadown and Dundalk. Running indicated that Bobby had given his fireman, Jimmy Croft, the driving hand. Nevertheless, it was great just to savour the occasion. Workings of empty coaches are not supposed to be run hard, and we did at least manage 56 mph after Lurgan. There were just a few minutes when, recovering from a permanent way slack at Knockmore, Bobby took the controls and *53* could probably have been heard in Dromore!

Saturday 31 May

The big day arrived; and an even bigger day for my younger brother Paul, who had just received word that morning that he would be joining me in Methody in the next school year. This was to be his first year; for me, in all probability, my last. So, as a bit of a celebration, I took him along for the fun.

I must digress a bit and go back four years. It is the last Saturday in August – traditionally in Northern Ireland called 'Black Saturday'. Each year, on this date, the Royal Black Institution parades in selected venues across the six counties. More recently the event has become synonymous with the end of the marching season. However, in 1965 there was little trouble or controversy surrounding the event. The Co Antrim demonstration was to be held in Lisburn, while in Co Armagh the venue would be Lurgan. So, for just a day, Lisburn hosted such steam that we almost forgot the atrocities committed in the name of progress just six months earlier (the closure of the Portadown to Derry line and the Newry and Warrenpoint branch). As well as Adelaide supplying a spate of steam trains bound for Lurgan and Portadown, York Road supplied three specials from Ballymoney, Ballymena and Antrim. These were handled by engines *1*, *10* and *6* respectively. Now engine number *1* was no stranger to Great Northern metals, but the others were. Paul accompanied me on my sightseeing trip that day and, in particular, got such a close view of *10* being cleaned and tended from the safe proximity of the loop platform, that she

Changing engines at Antrim – 51 prepares to leave for Portrush while 10 picks up a brake coach in the siding.

Engines off! Sunday school excursions seldom worked Portrush branch local trains, but 51 makes an exception with a four-coach train later that day. She is seen here at University halt heading for Coleraine.

The lore of gleaming preservation! Engine 171 arrives at Antrim with a RPSI special.

became a great favourite.

It was appropriate, therefore, that on this day of celebration, when the diesel stopped in Portadown, that the engine heading the seven-coach special should be number *10*. Mind you, as the late RM Arnold correctly notes, the running was far from celebratory. The uphill work was so bad that the 57 mph attained down the Maze was

flattering! The Antrim branch was restricted to 25 mph and although *10* and her crew did no more than 36 mph, some lost time was recovered. The picture on page 36 shows the scene at Antrim. We had to detrain some distance short of the platform, where *10* was replaced by *51* for the rest of the journey to Portrush. On the return, yet another engine would be waiting at Antrim to complete the journey. Consideration of coal capacity was the reason for this careful planning – a high bunk engine worked the Portrush section, while low bunk engines worked the Great Northern section.

I have not spoken of many regrets. Let's face it, in the summer of '69 I had mighty few. Not even my secret, unrequited, illicit love affair with a beautiful married woman (at least five years my senior!) yet fell into that category. Nonetheless, I do have some regrets about this day. I should have stayed with *51* to Portrush, instead of being wooed by the prospect of the RPSI's *171* on a Coleraine and Great Victoria Street special trip. Some aspects of *171*'s work that day were very satisfactory; but preservation is not what this book is about, nor was what I should have been about on the last Saturday in May 1969. There would be many more opportunities for *171* – for *51* and most of her sisters, time was fast running out. So I make no further mention of *171* and simply fast forward to 20.50 that evening, when I joined the real world again!

Almost to reinforce these sentiments, driver WJ Gillespie had *51* into Antrim so close to time that we had to check our watches. Now a number of enthusiasts had turned up, including Bob Hunter and the late Drew Donaldson, and I have to say we should all have been a little bit more subtle about how we boarded what, after all, was a private charter train! The engine supplied for the last stretch (this train had now involved four different engines!) was none other than number *6*, providing yet more similarities to that day four years before. The driver was Billy Montgomery – one of the younger Adelaide breed – whom I'd first noted on steam specials in 1966. In those days it was exceptional for anyone to be passed as driver below the age of 40, so Billy had probably 20 or so years driving diesels ahead of him – but not tonight! The band played 'Dizzy' as we made a rapid start out of Antrim and down to the Sixmilewater. Then a crusty old guard appeared and was perplexed by the task of how to sell us tickets over a closed (to passengers) stretch of line. Some enthusiasts were even chided that they should not have boarded at Antrim. I flashed my annual (Lisburn to Belfast) ticket and a day-return from Lisburn to Portadown, and he seemed content with that! Nothing, however, could reduce the sheer enjoyment of the occasion as *6* made a very competent run to Lisburn, bearing in mind the speed restriction. A speed of 42 mph was exceeded just before Glenavy and again at Legatiriff. Indeed, we were doing so well that, inevitably, we were stopped by signals at Knockmore Junction to allow a regular diesel through. Otherwise the 49-minute schedule would have been cut to just over 40. A quick shunt round the coaches at Lisburn and prospects for *6*'s first recorded mainline run on the GN looked good. Sadly this proved a false dawn, for only 51 mph was achieved at Moira and again at Kilmore. A brisk start out of Lurgan and 47 mph at Post 91 was all to no avail, for, at the very end of the day, some revellers decided to spoil the good behaviour by pulling the communication chord. So we were a few minutes late into Portadown, necessitating a swift run down the dank subway, which was such a feature of the old station, and then up onto the platform and into last diesel home.

Colour photographs of this day of steam activity appear on pages 45–8.

June 69

A new month often brings new challenges and this was certainly the case in June. The dawning of June was a stark reminder that public (and school) examinations lay only a matter of days away. My priorities were quite simple – all effort for the A' level in mathematics; spare some effort for physics, which had some common ground with the applied mathematical topics; and ignore chemistry, at least for this year!

Wednesday 4 June

There is only one explanation as to why I boarded the lunchtime 13.15 ex-Great Victoria Street at Adelaide – I'd sat Paper 1 in A' level Mathematics that morning and was now entitled to an afternoon off! The exam had gone well enough – but I still wasn't 'counting my chickens', for there were still two to go. This was the final year of a five-paper/four-subject system for Advanced level Mathematics in Northern Ireland. Under this system, the first three papers were 'pure', while papers 4 and 5 were 'applied'. My itinerary was papers 1, 2 and 4, which constituted A' level Mathematics, while 3 and 5 constituted Further Mathematics.

With papers in school exams in the mornings only, on the days immediately following, the remainder of the week was punctuated with lunchtime journeys home on different trains. Lisburn was well served with local trains at 12.20, 12.35, 12.50 and 13.01. The latter was non-stop to Finaghy, while the semi-fast 13.15 to Portadown stopped at Adelaide and Balmoral only. Return trains left Lisburn at 13.10, 13.25, 13.40 and 14.00 for the city. Such frequency was a throwback to the days when white-collared city executives had wives who stayed at home. These officials would often take a generous hour in the middle of the day and, if fortunate enough to live close to Balmoral, Finaghy or Dunmurry stations, might well consider going home for lunch. Today, all that has changed. Wives generally work – even in the upper social strata, and lunchtimes have largely been reduced to a sandwich at your desk, with the hope of getting away in reasonable time at the end of the day. Hence, there is no additional lunchtime traffic to speak of and the evening rush both starts and finishes earlier. There is not even the 'early closing' Wednesday, which ensured that lunchtime trains were well patronised for one day of the week.

Saturday 7 June

Another Saturday arrived, with more Sunday School excursions to Portrush. RJ (Batman) Simpson had number *4* with a ten-coach excursion booked out of York Road at 09.45. Much was expected, but like Bobby Quail on the previous week, RJ gave his fireman, Albert Plews, some driving practice. So speed fell to 16 mph at Monkstown and we recorded no more than 60 mph at Dunadry and again after Antrim, with a minimum of 42 mph at Post 26 (even worse climbing than poor steaming *51* had been guilty of two weeks earlier) and just 56 mph at Kellswater. The single-line work was no more inspirational – 50 mph was not exceeded until Post 48, 58 mph was attained before a signal check at Ballyboyland and 52 mph before the A26 road bridge slack.

A late start from Portrush on the return 19.15 provided the impetus to give the 'run of the day'.

Ballymena on 7 June 1969: Albert Plews attends to 4's replenishment while RJ (Batman) Simpson entertains an enthusiast on the footplate.

From the 'Right away!' RJ and *4* sounded like they meant business. The 330-ton train was away to 31 mph at Post 66, with 51 mph being exceeded on the branch before the customary signal check through Coleraine. Undeterred, we were away to 41 mph before the A26 slack. The slack was religiously observed, but for once a speed well into the mid-50s was recorded before Ballymoney, seldom the case with a heavy train. We roared through Ballymoney at the limit of 40 mph and never fell below 36 mph up the hill to Post 52. Thereafter the easing in Ballyboyland bank allowed RJ to race away to 42 mph at the signal-cabin, and never fall below 38 mph over Post 49. This was easily the best performance I ever had up Ballyboyland with a train of this size. Eventually Dunloy was reached no later than Harry's effort of three weeks earlier – but he had not had the handicap of a 14-minute late departure! So, the Londonderry-bound diesel was not kept waiting too long. We were away to 56 mph at Glarryford when RJ decided that he'd done enough, and possibly handed back control to the fireman, thereafter allowing the running to revert to the uninspiring stuff observed earlier

that day. Even so, he could not negate a very fine 53-minute timing from Portrush to Ballymena, with a heavy train and no less than five hand tablet or permanent way checks to contend with. The run on to Belfast was dull in the extreme, taking 46 minutes with no more than 56 mph at Kellswater, 58 mph after Cookstown Junction and a lazy 31 mph climb up the last three-mile stretch to Kingsbog. This was the sort of climb a multi-purpose diesel set would have made but, even with ten coaches, more was expected of number *4* and her crew! Nevertheless, as we got away to Kellswater and cast long shadows along the banks of the meandering waterways that punctuate the landscape around Ballymena, the band played on: 'Proud Mary keep on rollin'… rollin' like a river.'

Monday 9 June

Today I sat Paper 2 and had another run home on the 13.15. This was very much a repeat performance of the previous Wednesday. I'd like to think I'd get my 'A', but at this stage I travel hopefully rather than with certainty!

Wednesday 11 June

Summer (better known as examination) weather has arrived! Just to prove it, the railway line at Dunmurry buckled in the heat and caused disruption to homebound traffic.

Thursday 12 June

More good weather arrived with Paper 4 – the difference being that this was my one and only afternoon exam. So, while the sun beat down on the windows of the lecture hall, I got to grips with applied mathematics, A' level-style. 'What is this', I cried, for the NI examination board had delivered a gift – a paper of little more difficulty than might have been expected at O' level 'additional'. Notwithstanding the fact that easy papers are marked more stringently, or may have the required mark for the grade raised, I still reckoned that by 16.30 that day I had done enough – and that good news would await me on 4 August. Funny, when you get closer to the day of reckoning, such optimism tends to fade!

These, however, were not my thoughts on this perfect June day. After the exam I didn't want to go home, so I made my way to York Road. For almost three weeks NIR had been maintaining a very good record at keeping steam off the 17.30 to Larne – but this was my day and *51*, with a rake of largely ex-GN coaches, duly obliged. I was trying to preserve a little money – for there could yet be an expensive summer ahead, and covering the 'Sunday Schools' every week to Portrush was also eating into resources. The end of travel by steam train would come soon, but perhaps not that quickly. So I made use of the RPSI concessionary fare to Whitehead (introduced for members travelling to the RPSI site) and decided just to travel that far. This way one got two-thirds of the distance for well under half the price of a return to Larne, and that helped to eke out resources.

John McAuley was in charge that afternoon and he was a man of quite a nervous disposition. At one moment he could be providing a great run, then he would suddenly become nervous of speed and motion and would shut off steam – and even apply the brakes for no apparent reason! With a light five-coach load he was in reasonable form out to Carrickfergus, with 48 mph along the shore, a minimum of 39 mph before GreenIsland and 55 mph at Trooperslane. The run on to Whitehead was a bit dull – nothing more than 46 mph was attained in a lengthy eight and a half minutes for the section.

Unconfirmed reports were circulating that John had managed a heroic effort between Magheramorne and Ballycarry on the return journey. If so, enthusiasm had worn off by Whitehead. Number *51* exceeded 50 mph before Kilroot, but then a signal check at Downshire ruined any further prospects. The run up Mount bank would have been quite good if the engine hadn't been eased after attaining 38 mph at Trooperslane. More signal checks hampered progress and a maximum of 51 mph was recorded after Whitehouse. Even this was two mph more than the three-car AEC set managed before Lisburn on the 22.15 semi-fast. An engine out in *117* (*118* made up the other unit) was happening more and more frequently and was the cause of lax progress.

Saturday 14 June

No aid, in the form of a pilot engine, was offered to *53* or driver RJ (Batman) Simpson for the long rake of coaches which formed the 09.05 special to Portrush and which the engine now headed out of Platform 2. It proceeded slowly across the points and crossovers, taking over four minutes to reach Post 1. Then RJ started to work *53* quite hard and 45 mph was exceeded at Whitehouse. But even hard work was not enough and while 34–35 mph was held through Whiteabbey, speed then dropped off a little too dramatically on the 1/75 to Monkstown. As we approached the underbridge just before the station, with speed now down to just 12.5 mph, RJ chanced to look back down the train and counted the coaches. "One, two, ...ten, eleven – must be a mistake. Start again. One, two, ...ten, eleven!" Here, in the death throes of steam in the British Isles, the authorities had decided that it perfectly acceptable to send a train unaided to Kingsbog, carrying more than the maximum permitted load. This was faith indeed, for we estimated the weight behind the engine was 370 tons. Mind you, it wasn't only RJ who was taken by surprise. My logbook has the '0' in 10 over-written by a '1' – evidently I had made the same mistake! Mac Arnold also pretty well admits to the same in *NCC Saga*. The fireman that day was George Gaw and his version of the story was that the extra coach was not actually identified until they were heading down the bank towards Doagh! Anyway, whatever the truth, RJ opened *53* up a bit more and speed gradually started to recover – 13 mph at Mossley, 21 mph at Ballyclare Junction and 33 mph at Kingsbog. Thereafter he let 53 run a bit on the favourable terrain on to Ballymena. Sixty-five mph was attained at Dunadry, 56 mph into the dip after Antrim, a minimum of 49 mph up to MP26 and 61 mph at Kellswater. The 21¾ miles from passing Kingsbog to stopping in Ballymena took just over 24 minutes. Now why on earth I decided to leave this train at Ballymena I shall never know! Maybe it was fear that the intense load would lead to a poor run on the single line. Logically, this would be a more reasonable and understandable reaction when coming from Portrush, where the gradients are generally against the engine. But leave I did and Mac Arnold records that *53* and RJ were indeed in fine form the rest of the way to Portrush.

A long wait at Ballymena ensued, basking in the sun at the end of the down platform. At precisely 1.00 pm WJ Gillespie and *4* appeared on a late 11.50 special ex-York Road. It was just the standard ten-coach load, but *4* was distinctly dull, with nothing more than 54 mph down Ballyboyland. A shorter day in Portrush was followed by a repeat of the Saturday four weeks previous, with Harry Ramsey taking up the reins on the homebound 19.15. However, two things were different. Unlike *53*, *50* was making the first of what would be many appearances in Portrush that summer, while Mac Arnold was using his influence to edge a little more performance out of

Harry! Mind you, the cajoling didn't work over the first section to Dunloy, for once again Harry was prepared to take it easy until the 'dirty diesel' had been despatched. So another sub-25 mph run up Ballyboyland was assured! Even so, we actually had to stop and await the diesel. Then it was on to Ballymena with 52 mph at Glarryford and a livelier 55 mph round the Dunminning curves. But it was the section from Ballymena to the stop at the disused station of Doagh (where the Sunday School occupants would leave the train) which was the best. For once that year, a heavy train actually exceeded 60 mph at Kellswater and, despite a signal check at Milepost 26, again into the dip before Antrim. Number *50* was now being worked quite hard. So speed held above 48 mph right up to Milepost 15, where the engine was eased for the Doagh stop. Then, with an almost empty train, *50* was allowed to take it easy over the final stretch into York Road.

Tuesday 17 June

It was now under two weeks until term finished, when I would have much less reason to be on trains regularly frequented by the 'angel in blue'. I had pretty well decided that a forced stay of absence was necessary. In any case, she and her husband would likely be on holiday for some of the time and I would be occupied on the other side of the network! So, tonight was my last run on the 17.10 before the summer began in earnest. As usual, motive power was in the hands of a four-car BUT set. She, resplendent in a light blue summer frock and I, not so resplendent in a Methody uniform showing end-of-year signs of age, formed part of the crowd in rear car *122*. This car was a standard double ended BUT unit, with low back armchairs. If it hadn't been for the obvious attraction, I would certainly have chosen to travel in unit *129* at the front. This unit had been burnt out near the border with Éire, in a terrorist incident towards the end of the 1956–62 IRA campaign. At that time the Ulster Transport Authority (UTA) were just assembling the last of the MPD units (the

(Continued on page 49)

On the occasion of the first RPSI Open Day, 10 May 1969, NIR supplied steam on the 14.05 to Larne Harbour in the capable hands of No 5. In this view the train halts at Whitehead to deposit passengers heading for the Open Day.

Norman Johnston

Goraghwood or Dundalk next stop? The scene could easily have been five years earlier. No 53 has just arrived in Portadown with the empty coaches from Belfast on the evening of 30 May 1969.

Norman Johnston

No lack of steam – just a lack of using it! No 10 halts at Lurgan with the Portrush special on 31 May 1969.
Norman Johnston

The same train with No 10 taking water at Lisburn before reversing ends for the run to Antrim.
Norman Johnston

Jeep 51 with the excursion from Portadown on arrival at Portrush, 31 May 1969. To the right of the engine is the well-known Castle Erin holiday home.

Norman Johnston

No 4 taking water at Coleraine on 31 May 1969. Fireman Barney McCrory (now a NIR Inspector) keeps an eye on the photographer as well as his water supply. The area in the background is now an Ulsterbus garage.

Norman Johnston

Not the triple header that it seems! Nos 4 and 53 sit at Platform 2, Portrush, after taking water and will later join two return excursions back to Belfast, one of which is visible at Platform 1. The train at Platform 2 is the return Portadown excursion and will be hauled as far as Antrim by No 51, the last company steam train ever to work to Portadown in NIR days.

Norman Johnston

The scene at Antrim on the evening of 31 May 1969. On the left 51 prepares to run light engine back to York Road, while 6 moves gently forward from the former GN metals to pick up the excursion to Portadown.

Norman Johnston

(Continued from page 44)

double ended trio numbered *63–65*), and *129* was refurbished more akin to them. The car was given high back armchair seats, with maroon fabric and beige panelling. My granny, who lived in Belfast, always looked out for *129* when coming to visit us. Always one with an eye for a bargain, she used to say that it was like getting a first class seat for a second class price!

I don't record that there was an engine failed in either of the power-units, but progress that evening suggested this could have been the case. No doubt I was strutting around, drawing attention to myself by trying to find out what was the cause of the problem. If the 'angel in blue' was ever bemused by such adolescent antics, she never let it show. Progress was slow – 40 mph just managed before Dunmurry and over eight minutes taken was about a minute down on a reasonable run. Thereafter, just 41 mph before and 29 mph after the stop at Hilden continued to suggest that all was not well. Significantly, by the next morning NIR had strengthened the set to a five-car formation. Unit *126* was attached to *129*

and this set worked the 08.23 (Derriaghy and Dunmurry only) local to Belfast.

Saturday 21 June

Just two weeks of Northern Ireland's final steam Sunday School season remained. There were two excursions this week, compared with three on the previous week. The 09.05 excursion had *4* and Willie Gillespie in charge, with Barney McCrory firing. Obviously some lessons had been learned, because this train was given a pilot right through to Antrim – or perhaps the real reason was that the second excursion was starting from Antrim and would be composed of coaches stabled there. The pilot engine, *53*, was in the hands of Bertie Wright and a sharp run, with 51 mph at Whitehouse and speed holding the low 30s before a stop at Mossley, was achieved. The two engines had no difficulty starting away with 33 mph, before a signal stop halted progress at Kingsbog Junction. We all thought the pilot was coming off, but within a few seconds we were on our way again. An easy run for two engines produced 68mph through Dunadry and still had us in

Nos 53 *and* 4 *double head the ten-coach special into Antrim on 21 June 1969.*

49

Engine 4 *awaits the all clear at Cullybackey with the 09.05 special from York Road.*

Together again. A branch path is saved by dispensing 53 *and* 4 *together – seen here approaching Coleraine bunk first on 21 June 1969.*

Antrim, with a total running time of just 31 minutes despite two stops and a further signal check. Reduced to one engine, a good run to Ballymena ensued, with 48 mph up to Milepost 26 and 62 mph at Kellswater and a time of under 16 minutes, notwithstanding the slow stop to position the engine by the water column. The single line produced somewhat duller running, with 52 mph at Glarryford, 54mph down Ballyboyland and again at Macfin. The Portstewart (later Cromore) loop was switched in and progress along the branch was sedate.

Gillespie and *4* were also in charge of the earlier 18.45 return excursion. Some lively running was at times ruined by another problem. The ten-coach train contained some of the older ex-GN wooden bodied coaches, and these vehicles occasionally had sticking brakes. Such was the case this day. Gillespie started well out of Portrush with 31 mph at Milepost 66, but the first bout of sticking brakes halted the train during the hand tablet exchange at Portstewart. A solid pound up the hill out of Coleraine preceded the same thing happening, when braking for the A26 bridge slack. So it was third time lucky through Ballymoney and we hammered up Ballyboyland bank with 38 mph at the cabin and a minimum of 34 mph at Milepost 49. After passing through Dunloy, nothing more than 52 mph was attained at Glarryford. Then came the water-stop at Ballymena and just 55 mph at Kellswater, though speed did stay above 50 mph over Milepost 26 and 60 mph was just touched into the dip before Antrim. Thereafter Gillespie was always about two mph behind Harry Ramsey's fine run of the previous week. Even this would have suggested that over 40 mph would be held over the summit. This week we would not be rescued by a Doagh stop and *4* became somewhat winded over the last three miles, with speed eventually falling to 37 mph. Thereafter stops at Mossley and more brake problems ensured leisurely progress into the terminus. The run home that evening had something of a school flavour to it, for further down the coach I could observe a young Classics' teacher wrestling with a Sunday School class of 11-year-olds. With each unscheduled stop they seemed to become more boisterous! The young teacher was Wilfred Mulryne, who would eventually rise to the position of headmaster in Methodist College, one of Northern Ireland's most prestigious schools.

And the band played on: 'Baby make it soon… I can't wait another day…'

Sunday 22 June

While I had been enjoying the delights of steam at the seaside on the previous day, my mother had also departed for coastal places, taking with her my grandmother who, now well into her seventies, had been campaigning for an accompanied holiday for some time! That left a trio of 'men' at home and my father, always willing to try something new, produced some tinned Italian meatballs in tomato sauce for lunch. This was still a time when most of us hardly knew where the continent was, never mind eat their style of food. And to this day I have never again countenanced tinned Italian meatballs in tomato sauce!

Monday 23 June

I was violently sick for the first time just after midnight struck – experiencing classic food poisoning symptoms – vomiting every hour on the hour until morning. Later Paul joined in with similar symptoms. Much later that morning, after my father had gone to 'school' (he was a head teacher by profession), and as I dragged bedclothes out for washing, which had unfortunately got in the way of stereophonic projectile vomit, I felt every bone in my body hurt.

But it is amazing how fast you recover when you're young. By later that evening I was eating simple food and had even cycled down to Lisburn station. There I made a trip into Belfast, with the four-car BUT set which had likely formed the 17.10 earlier that day. Not for the first time that year, the 'angel in blue' had been transported home in car *121*!

Tuesday 24 June

Midsummer's day was a day of sport. Firstly, the school sports were held at Pirrie Park early that evening. I was entered for the two-lap 880 yards – this was the last time that that specific distance would be run at Methody – by next year it would be replaced by the 'metric' 800 metres. The first lap went quite well – I made the bell in 65 seconds and was still looking good for a chance of a minor place. Then, untypical for me, as I usually had a good finish, the 'wheels came off' and I took a laborious and unflattering 73 seconds for the second lap and finished nowhere. The previous day's trauma had taken its toll, particularly when I switched from aerobic to anaerobic breathing halfway through the race. My father praised me for a good fight against the odds. Strangely, it would be nearly a quarter century before I again attempted this distance when, as a veteran aged 41, I would better the two minutes ten seconds barrier which I had just about considered achievable that evening.

Wimbledon fortnight had started on Monday, and later that evening we were enthralled by a match that so clearly demonstrated the idea of veteran fortitude. This is documented in the Guinness book of records as the longest singles match ever staged and took place between Charlie Pasarell and Pancho Gonzales. After a marathon first set to Gonzales (24–22), Pasarell easily took the second 6–1. The third set was another mammoth struggle and was played out against lengthening evening shadows. We picked up the coverage late into that set. My father, himself then aged 47, expressed great sympathy for veteran Gonzales. In the fading light, he felt the umpire should have called time when, for reasons of age and acute eyesight, there was a clear disadvantage to the older man. He was right. In the mounting gloom, Gonzales eventually lost 16–14 to go two sets to one down. The match resumed on the next day, when my father would have gone to see my grandfather and his sister-in-law, Auntie Mae, in Bangor. Now Auntie Mae was a great tennis enthusiast and very 'modern' for a lady of 75. Just prior to the start of the 1969 Wimbledon season, she had become one of the first people in Northern Ireland to possess a colour television. So the next afternoon they witnessed, in glorious technicolour,

Gonzales come back to take the last two sets – but not before another long final set, won 11–9. The sheer effort probably contributed to him losing in the next round and this match, more than any other, heralded the introduction of tie-breaks in all but the final set.

Wednesday 25 June

Today was a school day with a difference. Instead of normal classes, those in lower sixth who were studying science subjects had been invited to an introduction day at the New University in Coleraine. So that morning, when I came out of Great Victoria Street station, I turned left instead of right! We boarded the 09.45 to Portrush and Londonderry. This was not a 'crack' train and was typically rostered to a six-car MPD set. The increasing lack of reliability of these units meant that York Road shed had plumped for a four power-car, two trailers arrangement. Even so, we still fell to 26 mph at Mossley, something that could easily be bettered by a six-coach steam train.

Now I was not intending to make the New University one of my top university choices, but was quite impressed with their pure sciences and the ambience of a campus university. So, while all my other choices eventually were for Mathematics or Statistics, I kept one fallback position of Physics at Coleraine.

A useful visit over, we boarded the branch train at University and then transferred to the 15.00 ex-Londonderry at Coleraine. Motive power was a six-car Hampshire unit (power cars *72* and *75*), stretched to seven by the addition of an extra trailer. This would have tempered running a little (speeds in the mid-80s were commonplace with these new units), though arrival at York Road's Platform 3 was one minute before time. This was just in time to observe a rake of six steam coaches sitting in Platform 2 and awaiting the departure of the 17.30 to Larne Harbour!

So I said 'Cheerio' to my schoolmates, purchased a return to Larne Harbour, and joined my enthusiast colleagues for what was to be the first in a long sequence of runs on the 17.30. Soon number *4* appeared with the redoubtable Dan

McAtamney in charge. Now while Dan was sparing about working an engine hard, he could always be counted on to make a good start, run down a hill and leave braking until the last possible minute! This night's run enveloped all these qualities, and was also a fair illustration of the steam-hauled 17.30 in good form. Just as Pancho Gonzales won his marathon, we were away to Milepost 1 (Crusaders FC) in under three minutes, just touched 50 mph at Whitehouse and fell to 40 mph at Whiteabbey. Then we held 44 mph over Greenisland, raced away to 64 mph down 'the Mount' and made a neat stop in Carrickfergus in just 14 m 16 s from Belfast. Another good start out of Carrick and 58 mph round the reverse curves had us in Whitehead in 7 m 5 s. At this stage, a three-minute deficit leaving York Road had been cut to just one minute late. Then it took just under four minutes to reach Ballycarry (maximum 48 mph) and ten minutes and 16 seconds on to Larne, with 50 mph before Magheramorne loop and 56 mph at the Glynn – more solid work.

The run home was not as bright, as was so often the case with this train. However, Dan did achieve 57 mph at Downshire Park and a time of 7 m 30 s from Whitehead to Carrickfergus. The uphill work was similar to John McAuley's effort earlier that month, but 44 mph on the stretch between Greenisland and Jordanstown and 58 mph along the the shore, after the Whiteabbey stop, were distinctly brighter.

Thursday 26 June

With the school year nearly over, I could afford to take my fast fleeting hobby a little more seriously! So it was back to York Road, where this evening Dan had *50* and a load of six coaches and a van on the 17.30. I should point out that four-wheeled vans were generally restricted to 45 mph, which makes the ensuing run all the more amazing! A speed of just 49 mph at Whitehouse followed a very sharp start to Seaview. Then Dan did well to hold 41 mph at Whiteabbey, produced 47 mph into the dip through Jordanstown and held 45 mph at Greenisland. His time to pass the latter was 10 m 14 s – well up with my best runs on this train. On account of the van, we all thought he would shut off steam and trundle down the hill to Carrick, where he would still have held time – not a bit of it! Dan raced away to no less than 67 mph through the Mount and made an even fiercer stop in Carrick than on the previous evening, to arrive in 13 m 38 s from Belfast. Although he only did 54 mph round the Whitehead curves, the time of 7 m 6 s was almost identical to Wednesday's effort.

For the run home, *50* now had six coaches and two four-wheeled vans. Running was generally duller than the previous evening, though 57 mph in the lough shore and a time of 4 m 29 s from Whiteabbey to pass Seaview, before a signal stop outside the terminus halted progress, was worth noting.

Friday 27 June

So far that week Dan had had engines that would still have been regarded as fairly good mechanically. Then on Friday evening, York Road Shed produced number *6*. Despite another very good start to Seaview, and not having any vans to contend with, the difference soon became apparent. Dan could only manage 45 mph at Whitehouse and was down to 31 mph at Whiteabbey. The acceleration to 38 mph through Jordanstown just about held up to the Greenisland platform, but he almost made up the lost time by a spirited 63 mph through 'the Mount' and another blistering stop into Carrickfergus, netting a time of 15 m 17 s. A time of 7 m 32 s on to Whitehead, with 53 mph round the curves, was commendable enough, even if it was somewhat down on the performances of *4* and *50*.

At this stage I was still conserving money by only going as far as Whitehead on RPSI concessionary tickets, priced at 3s 6d (17.5p) for adults and 2s (10p) for juniors. The drawback was that it was nearly an hour and three quarters before the return train. Mind you, there are few nicer places than Whitehead for a stroll along the prom, or a wander round the small town. And there were always 'spoil' trains to observe or photograph. So, by 7.00 pm I was back at the station when, instead of viewing a 'spoil' train, the sight of number *5* hauling a failed three-car MPD set entertained me. This train was actually the delayed 18.15 ex-Larne Harbour and it meant that two return trains in sequence from Larne Harbour would be steam-hauled. Harry Ramsey was on board 5's footplate and clearly enjoying himself, much to the railcar driver's acute embarrassment. There was some gurgling and spluttering from one of the power cars (38 or 45), but apparently this was sufficient only to raise the brake off the railcar set. Harry was quite determined to produce a more competent run home than the MPD set would have produced even if it had been working in its entirety! Certainly 55 mph at Kilroot and 6 m 48 s to stop in 'the Barn' was competent stuff, as were the two short sections on to Carrickfergus and Clipperstown. For a stopping train, 31 mph between Clipperstown and Trooperslane and over 32 mph on the next section to Greenisland was actually very good. Things were taken gently to Jordanstown and Whiteabbey, after which Harry just shaded 60 mph in the lough shore, before a signal stop outside York Road. This was better than the railcar indeed!

Saturday 28 June

The last ever steam 'Sunday School' Saturday had arrived. Readers will possibly have noted that so far all of the remaining eight engines had played a part in the 1969 season, albeit number 5 had only had a cameo appearance on the fine double-headed run of the first Saturday, while 6 and 10 were only involved in the GN excursion. This accounts for all the engines except one, for number 55 had worked very few passenger trains since 14 December 1968, when she had given an uncharacteristically poor performance on the train chartered by the Rev Ian Paisley to meet the return of the *Clyde Valley* gun-running ship at Larne Harbour. Things were almost rectified upon departure of the 10.10 special from York Road. This later path was to enable Sunday Schools from the Carrickfergus area to join the train and they had arrived courtesy of a special with driver Bertie Wright, engine number 6 and nine coaches. For Portrush a further two coaches were added, making another eleven-coach train. Engine number 50 was

allocated to the task and a pilot to Kingsbog, in the shape of number 5, was gratefully received. (While for a few miles we had $50 + 5 = 55$, the engine in question actually made it to Portrush for the first time in over a year on another excursion.) Driver Davie McDonald and pilot driver RJ Simpson got away in fine style, with 55 mph at Whitehouse, speed staying above 28 mph on the Mossley bank and a time to stop in Kingsbog of 15 m 43 s. Now the real test began. 50 could be a grand engine, and for this reason she tended to be York Road's third choice (after 4 and 53) for any passenger duties that season. On other occasions she could be a steam-shy stubborn pig of an engine. The run down to Antrim was worthy of the former description – with 66 mph momentarily exceeded at Dunadry. The cold start out of Antrim with such a big load was not easy and speed just touched 41 mph before Milepost 26. However, 58 mph at Kellswater and under 17 minutes to Ballymena was tolerable in the circumstances. A valiant start up through Cullybackey with 36 mph at Post 37, 49 mph round the Dunminning curves and 51 mph at Glarryford was in a similar vein and we were away to 58 mph when the emergency brake was suddenly applied at Ballyboyland. Apparently the floor collapsed in the Guard's apartment of the rear coach, which was an old wooden bodied ex-Great Northern composite-brake. So we sat for ten minutes while planks were replaced in the floor of the coach. Some damage appeared to have been done to the vacuum system for, when we eventually started to move again, it was a case of limping along all the rest of the way to Portrush. The fact that Davie couldn't even run down the hill suggested strongly that the brakes were dragging very badly. This delay then cost us our advertised path on the branch and we sat for a further 22 minutes in Coleraine. So the final Sunday School excursion, which just seventeen easy miles from Portrush had looked set to run into the seaside terminus by midday, arrived instead at 12.46. The mishap had cost each person on that train at least three-quarters of an hour's enjoyment in Portrush.

Of all of the engines described herein, 55 was my favourite. From the first time I'd noticed her,

Last steam 'Sunday school' Saturday. No 50 arrives with empty coaches from Coleraine, 51 prepares to leave with the 18.45 and 55 awaits departure of the 19.15 special on 28 June 1969.

on the return 14.45 ex-Dublin (16.00 ex-Dundalk) in late 1964, she had a habit of producing great runs. In 1966 she produced some stirring stuff with the Adelaide drivers on the former GN section. Transferred to the NCC section, after Adelaide closed in November 1966, I again had some fine runs with her in 1967 and during Easter 1968. She was something of an old workhorse and certainly had had her fair share of heavy spoil trains. From mid-1968 York Road considered her to be too 'rattled out' to be worthy of passenger trains, and from then on she became more enigmatic that number *5*! But she wasn't going to go down without a fight and for the last few weeks that regular passenger steam working remained, *55* would in her own quiet way leave her mark.

My last ever Sunday School excursion from Portrush turned out to be the one and only time that I had to contend with 11 coaches on a Portrush to Belfast train. This dubious assignment was handed to a 'rattled out' engine that had only worked a couple of Larne-line passenger trains since the *Clyde Valley* excursion! Then, as now, the driver was WJ Gillespie, a driver whose style of

running probably most reflected the state of the engine and not his own state! It was not without some trepidation that I chose this run home – I could have sampled more of *50*'s delights. I so much feared that *55* would be dreadful and I so much wanted something better. Well, it was a slow start up the 1/76 to Dhu Varren, with 26 mph at Post 66 and then the hand tablet exchange at Portstewart. Given that, 46 mph at the University was commendable. The A26 bridge slack ensured no more than 47 mph before Ballymoney. Gillespie took the slack through the station at 32 mph and then never fell below 30 mph all the way up the steepest part of the bank. He was away to 36 mph at Ballyboyland cabin and finally held 33 mph at Post 49. By now, I was starting to believe that *55* was far from finished! Dunloy (and the diesel) despatched with, 50 mph was just exceeded at Glarryford and again before Cullybackey. So, by Ballymena the single line section was over. That was always going to be a struggle, with a train of this size, and Gillespie had dealt with it with competence.

Well watered, *55* got under way for Belfast.

Fifty-six mph was achieved at Kellswater, 49 mph up to Post 26 and 55 mph before Antrim, passed in just one second under the 15-minute schedule. Then we started to get a flavour of the true *55*. I'm sure if anyone was on the platform at Antrim that evening, they would have been able to hear the engine some four minutes later when, approaching Dunadry, we were still doing 54 mph. The steep section of the bank (Post 17.5) then pulled speed down to 46 mph, but we recovered to 47 mph through and beyond Templepatrick. Even by Doagh speed was still registering 43 mph. We never fell below 40 mph and roared past Kingsbog cabin at 41 mph. This would have been considered good running with ten coaches – with 11 it was brilliant. We could now afford to take it easy down the bank, with nothing more than 56 mph at Mossley and 52 mph on the lough shore. For a run which completely lacked any big speed, this was sheer competence and the time of 41 m 14 s in from Ballymena was well below that booked. Good ol' *55*! She'd been given one chance to redeem herself and she'd passed with flying colours. You could almost here the conversation later down the shed: "See that oul' *55* engine – she was in great form coming home from Portrush. Maybe we should give her a few more passenger outings." And that is precisely what they did!

The day was not over yet. The Carrickfergus contingent still had to be taken home. This was accomplished by splitting the train, just arrived, between the third and fourth coaches, resulting in John McAuley and number *6* having a train of eight coaches for the run out to Carrickfergus. As might be expected, this was not conducive to speed, with nothing more than 41 mph out the lough shore and stops at Greenisland and Trooperslane. And so, at 22.05 that evening, the last steam-hauled Sunday School excursion reached its final destination.

Strangely, a song to mark this day did not manifest itself until nearly five years later when the Eagles released their third album, entitled 'On the Border'. On that album is a song, albeit written about a 1955 Chevrolet, whose lyrics are so appropriate to the occasion. The song is the Tom Waits-penned 'Ol' '55'!

Here, another interesting connection arises. Sarah McLaughlan is a relatively new singer/songwriter who, even as I write this, hasn't really 'broken' in Britain. Strangely, 'Ol' '55' is one of the very few songs, not written by herself, that she has recorded. Why do I mention this and why should it be interesting? Because from this lady I obtained the best line to sum up how I felt and how I approached life that summer – particularly in the early summer. It was, as she expresses in the song 'Wait' (from the album 'Fumbling Towards Ecstasy') that "it was like the new born hope – unjaded by the years".

Monday 30 June

This was the first day of complete freedom from school and a typical Northern Ireland summer's day – cool, grey clouds and threatening rain! At least the 17.30 was again steam-hauled, and what engine did York Road come up with this time? Correct – number *55*! With Percy Mitchell on the footplate, the combination of engine and driver was exactly the same as my first (and best) ever experience with this train. The load, at seven coaches, was just about as much as the Larne line could cope with before one really started to experience poorer running. *55* took the first mile rather gingerly; thereafter the run to Carrick was fine, with 49 mph at Whitehouse, 42 mph at Whiteabbey, 47 mph into the Jordanstown dip and then holding 46 mph up to Greenisland. The run down the Mount did produce 60 mph and the time of 15 m 2 s, to stop in Carrickfergus exactly to schedule. A time of 7 m 19 s on to Whitehead, with 59 mph round the reverse curves, was also commendable. As noted before, Percy would not run as hard on the homebound train. Even so, 51 mph was attained before an unscheduled stop at the diminutive and staggered platform of 'Eden'. The run up the hill from Carrickfergus to Greenisland just exceeded 37 mph at Trooperslane, while he managed 55 mph on the section in from Whiteabbey along the lough shore.

July '69

Tuesday 1 July

A new month, but with a very similar pattern to the previous day, bringing my count of consecutive steam-runs on the 17.30 to five. This evening Percy had 53 and one less coach than on the previous night. This led to even better running, with 55 mph at Whitehouse, and 45 mph at Whiteabbey. We then touched 50 mph into the Jordanstown dip and held 46 mph over Greenisland. For just the third time in my life I recorded a sub-ten minute time to pass the latter. We were now actually in danger of running early, so Percy shut off steam down the Mount (maximum 56 mph) and still arrived in Carrickfergus in a fine time of 13 m 57 s. On to Whitehead and a time of 7 m 20 s (maximum speed 55 mph) was not quite as good as the previous evening, but still highly commendable.

The run home produced a time of 7 m 38 s to Carrickfergus and 58 mph at Downshire Park. Uphill the engine was again worked easily with just 38 mph exceeded at Trooperslane. A speed of 43 mph and an under three minute timing to Jordanstown was satisfactory, and the final section from Whiteabbey produced 54 mph on the lough shore.

Wednesday 2 July

On the day that Brian Jones of the Rolling Stones died, I had a decision to make. So far I'd been conserving cash by just travelling as far as Whitehead. If the daily occurrence of steam-hauled evening business expresses continued, then I would be better purchasing a seven-day rail runabout and 'going where I pleased' (i.e. through to Larne Harbour). In the event, I would have been better buying this ticket the previous Saturday,

using it to Portrush that day and then through to Larne on Monday and Tuesday. Funny how we can always be so smart in retrospect! Anyway, once I'd confirmed steam on the 17.30, I bit the bullet and purchased my first rail runabout of the '69 summer season.

It was to be another turn for number 55 – almost a regular, this engine! And another good run too. Starting steadily at just 52 mph at Whitehouse and 42 mph at Whiteabbey, we then were up to over 47 mph into the dip and held 45 mph to Greenisland (passed in 10 m 21 s). Since we weren't running so early tonight, a swifter descent produced 61 mph at the Mount and a good time of 14 m 8 s to Carrickfergus. The Whitehead section was covered in 7m 8 s, with speed momentarily above 55 mph round the curves. Running at 47 mph before the Ballycarry stop (reached in 4 m 8 s) was also solid work. The section on to Larne Town, completed in just three seconds under 11 minutes, would have been faster had it not been for the somewhat unusual decision of routing us through the slow loop at Magheramorne (taken at 21 mph). Notwithstanding this, 55 achieved over 50 mph before the slack and got away to 56 mph through the Glynn.

The run home, though again taken easily was slightly better than previous evenings. Firstly, Percy actually exceeded 30 mph between the Harbour and Town stations – a feat not often achieved! Then we actually touched 40 mph before the Glynn stop. Slightly less worthy of note were maximum speeds of 41 mph, 48 mph and 34 mph on the sections to Magheramorne, Ballycarry and Whitehead respectively. Reaching Carrickfergus in 7 m 29 s (maximum 57 mph) was similar to the previous evening, but 40 mph at Trooperslane was better, with Greenisland reached in 5 m 58 s, as was exceeding 56 mph on the lough shore.

In just five days *55* had worked three trains and proved she could still run with the best.

Thursday 3 July

Seven not out! Seven sequential days of steam on the 17.30 – it seemed it could last forever! A further bonus tonight was that I would actually record a run with number *5* without another engine being involved! As with every evening (except Monday) the standard six-coach load was in play. Now, in comparison with the other two engines, *5* did show some weakness, but it was just so nice to record this enigmatic machine. The run out to Carrickfergus was slower, with just over 48 mph out the Shore, falling to 40 mph at Whiteabbey and again before GreenIsland. A maximum of 57 mph through the Mount produced a time to Carrickfergus of 15 m 20 s. We also took a lengthier 7 m 42 s on to Whitehead, but our maximum speed (54 mph) was not so dissimilar to other evenings. Reaching just 44 mph before Ballycarry, an unfortunate incident befell fireman Dave Smith – his shovel broke in two! This meant no more fuelling, so Percy would need to preserve steam a little on the section to Larne. Like the previous evening we were routed through the slow loop at Magheramorne, and 47 mph before and 51 mph after the slack produced a time to Larne just 24 seconds longer than that occasion. At the Harbour we all surrounded driver and fireman and much joviality was made about the incident. A replacement shovel was eventually found.

For the run home an extra (maximum 45 mph) van was added. Percy made a reasonable effort with 38 mph before Glynn, 41 mph before Magheramorne and 49 mph before Ballycarry. The difficult Whitehead section produced 34 mph and we touched 56 mph through Downshire, reaching Carrickfergus in 7 m 39 s. The uphill work was weaker, with just 37 mph at Trooperslane, but over 57 mph on the lough shore was commendable and York Road was reached just one minute late. Tonight had attracted a fair smattering of enthusiasts – indeed NIR will never realise how much revenue was lost when this train ceased being steam-hauled, while the incident with the shovel had led to an almost carnival atmosphere. Somewhere the band played 'Bringing on back the good times...'

Friday 4 July

The next day the atmosphere should have been carnival but wasn't. A large group of 'Orange' bandsmen were due to go over to Scotland for the Glasgow 'mini Twelfth'. So the 13.50 boat train needed to be strengthened and this was achieved by substituting a nine-coach steam train for the usual three-coach diesel. I'm afraid I always found such occasions somewhat oppressive and daunting – you never knew when one of these boys would suddenly take umbrage. Nine coaches on the Larne line is not a good idea – it was even less of a good idea when the engine rostered was number *5*! The man in charge was Bobby Vance of Larne. Right away this run was a disaster. We made a late start and then had to stop to pick up employees at Greencastle. This ruined any chance of a run out the lough shore. Speed fell to 23 mph at Whiteabbey, making the 32 mph sustained up to Post 6 almost look glamourous by comparison. We actually touched 48 mph down the Mount and, after the Barn stop, 47 mph round the Whitehead curves was 'as good as it got!' There was some indication of communication chord pulling (typical of the clientele), and the resulting sticking brakes meant that the section to Ballycarry took over six minutes (maximum 39 mph). The same speed was achieved before the Magheramorne stop. Unfortunately this station happens to sit on a short but steep 1/64 grade. Now, *5*'s valves were badly set and this problem was compounded by the fact that her boiler pressure had been reduced to 175 psi. So poor Vance spent seven minutes teasing the engine into a position of maximum tractive effort in order to get the train restarted. By the time we reached Larne Harbour the boat was close to sailing, but had of course been held for the worthy troop about to be unleashed upon it.

The return working for the 13.50 boat train was the 15.20 all stations (except Mount) from Larne Harbour to Belfast. The 15.20 was known as the 'school train' – it was a pity for the usual clientele that it was steam-hauled in the first week of the school holidays! Already poor progress outwards had ensured a fifteen minute late departure for the city-bound train. Unlike airports, NIR never made ludicrously stupid announcements like 'NIR regrets to inform passengers that the 15.20 all stations to Belfast has been delayed for reasons of the late arrival of the inbound train!'

Now while this melee was in progress, Ann Jones was completing the unusual feat of winning the ladies' singles title for Britain at Wimbledon.

Al Robinson's brother Bobby was given the task of getting us home, and probably received some well-timed advice from Vance, who was now booking-off for the day. A telephone call to Magheramorne signal cabin (where the spoil trains were loaded) would have gone unnoticed by the few enthusiasts present. We got under way with Robinson doing his best, just exceeding 32 mph before Glynn and 34 mph before Magheramorne. A quarter of a mile further on and we unexpectedly stopped again at the loop. Now spoil trains used two engines – if one was steaming badly the second could always compensate. So 5 was returned to 'spoil' duties while a different engine was added. And which engine was that? You just might have guessed – 55! Suddenly old drab 55 was becoming a bit of a celeb'! Right away the running improved – not spectacularly, but we did mange 41 mph before Ballycarry. Some hard work up the hill to Whitehead gave a speed of over 32 mph. We almost touched 45 mph before the Kilroot stop and on this section actually gained a minute against booked time (5 m 47 s from Whitehead). The cluster of little stations and halts around Carrickfergus meant that Robinson had to work 55 very hard at all times. So there was great 'stir' along the seafront as quite sharp sectional running was made on to Eden, Downshire Park, Barn,

Carrickfergus and Clipperstown. It was an interesting spectacle logistically too, for at that time Eden, Downshire Park and Clipperstown were short halts, built to accommodate only the first coach of a train. Usually this meant that intending passengers travelled in the first coach of three. Today they had to make sure they were housed in the first coach of nine! Starting nine coaches up through the Mount was a fairly daunting task, but surefooted 55 exceeded 25 mph before both of the Trooperslane and Greenisland stops. Down the hill at 39 mph before Jordanstown was good, followed by two more 'little sections' to Bleach Green and Whiteabbey. The last section along the lough shore was well handled, with 53 mph and a very good stop into York Road to net a time of 7 m 16 s.

There was just one thing missing at York Road – there were no steam coaches at Platform 2. What with the earlier troubles of the day, resulting in two engines being involved in the train just arrived at Platform 3, the shed had, successfully, made a special effort to find a diesel. The chain (of steam on the 17.30) was broken and would remain so for some time.

Saturday 5 July

What's this! I've got the time and I've got the ticket and this 'darn' railway don't have the trains! The 07.55 and 14.05 (Saturdays) boat trains were supposed to be steam-hauled, but since the 'July fortnight' doesn't actually begin until next week, NIR sneaked diesels onto both turns.

Sunday 6 July

Today I'm bound for a different destination. Welcome back to Belfast's third railway terminus – that of the former Belfast and County Down Railway at Queen's Quay. In the 1960s nothing was sacred on Northern Ireland's railways. Lines could be removed simply because they got in the way of a road building programme. So, while steam engines on the Larne line laboured day and night, laying the foundations for a new motorway, the line to Bangor was completely self-contained because its link to the outside world (via the

Central line) had been in the way of a road-widening scheme at Middlepath Street. This remained the case from August 1965 until the closure of Queen's Quay and establishment of Belfast Central Station, in April 1976.

One of the problems of isolation was that sufficient stock had to be maintained at Queen's Quay to permit all normal activities. This included locomotive (or in this case diesel railcar) workshops. Even railway maintenance in the form of ballast trains etc. had to be run by diesel power cars, detached from the normal trailers, hauling loaded wagons.

The complete motive power for the Bangor line amounted to just 16 Multi-Engined Diesel (MED) cars, together with a similar number of intermediate trailers, some of which were merely converted non-corridor coaches. On most weekday mornings and evenings it was normal for 12 of these cars to be in service. At any time one or two cars would be undergoing an overhaul, so there was little room for failure. Credit is due to the Queen's Quay fitters, but they always did seem to fare better at keeping cars in service than did their colleagues at York Road. Power cars allocated to the Bangor line were numbered *14–17* (which had bodies built from old coaches), together with the entire set of newly constructed frames, numbered *24–35*.

On this particular day I was using my runabout ticket to go down and visit my grandfather and aunt in Bangor.

The 13.20 ex-Queen's Quay was in the hands of a three-car unit with *25* and *30* as power cars. As far as Cultra this unit proved what was generally true about the BCDR-based MEDs – they were every bit as strong as today's three-car 80-class or 450-class units! Certainly, exceeding 55 mph between Sydenham and Holywood and away to 37 mph through Marino would be par for the course. Then an engine cut out and we were down to 33 mph at Craigavad and only managed 50 mph before the Helen's Bay stop. The 14.20 ex-Queen's Quay had a four-car formation in the hands of cars *24* and *29*. This was a mighty old struggle – the extra trailer could do that. No more

than 47 mph was achieved between Sydenham and Holywood. Speed never rose above 30 mph as we mounted the 1/73 to Craigavad, where a signal stop was followed by extra stops at the new stations of Seahill and Crawfordsburn Hospital and ensured that we were some seven minutes late into the seaside terminus.

With the visit over, the 20.00 ex-Bangor was formed by a three-car MED with power cars *32* and *33*. (Quite often the sets would work in sequential number formation, with the smaller even-numbered cars pointing towards Bangor.) NIR were then in the process of providing the MEDs with four-speed gear boxes, but my recollection is that *32* and *33* had not yet had the transformation from the old torque conversion system. Certainly the run home was typical of the old MED mode, with 61 mph through Marino (only facilitated by shutting power off down the hill!), the 'standard' 53 mph between Holywood and Sydenham and a couple of minutes lost against the tight 25 minute/five stops timing in from Bangor.

Monday 7 July

So why am I back on the Bangor line again? For the second day running I'm on the 13.20 ex-Queen's Quay, with the three-car MED set comprising cars *25* and *30*. Almost certainly the explanation goes as follows. My aunt will have needed some work done to the garden or, more likely, to the guttering of her bungalow. I suspect the latter, for in those days one would not have been seen cleaning gutters on a Sunday! So I've obviously returned to attend to the task. A little over two hours later and I return to Bangor station to board the 16.05 for Belfast, pockets no doubt swollen with silver, for my aunt was never ungenerous in her appreciation of a task well done!

The outward journey had been most notable for the 51 mph on the short section between Seahill and Helen's Bay and proves beyond a shadow of a doubt that *25/30* had received the four-speed gearbox conversion. Anchor three-car set *34/35* formed the 16.05 and produced a run home somewhat better than that of a typical 450-class. Again, there is no doubt that this set possessed the four-speed gearboxes. A swift descent from Seahill and 66 mph through Marino was just about the highest speed I had recorded with these units on the Bangor line. Fifty-nine mph between Holywood and Sydenham was also worthy of note.

I made my way across to York Road where it was driver Jimmy Simpson's week on the 17.30. Jimmy differed from many of his colleagues – he did not like steam engines unless they were performing impeccably! No doubt he had remonstrated with York Road shed to find him a diesel, and the shed had duly obliged. In fact, all week long they obliged. It was just as well I'd used my runabout ticket to earn some 'readies', for I was getting precious little steam use out of it!

Once it became clear that no steam engine was going out on the Larne line, I decided to take a diesel run to Portrush. It had turned into a lovely summer's evening and it seemed a shame not to make something out of this 'millstone'. The 18.00 ex-York Road was one of the 'crack' Londonderry trains and was composed of a six-car Hampshire set (with power cars *72* and *75*). The branch train at Coleraine was untypically a four-car MED set, with motive power supplied by cars *9* and *12*, and this set would also work the 19.55 to Belfast. Interestingly, this would be my only run with a non-steam train on the 19.55 that summer. Cars *9* and *12* had already received the four-speed conversions and at first the run home was better than one might have believed possible by a MED set! We managed a 44–45 mph run up Ballyboyland and touched 65 mph at Glarryford. After Ballymena we touched 66 mph at Kellswater. It was after Antrim, where steam engines finally show their mettle and diesels have nothing left to give, that things came apart. Away to just 46 mph at Dunadry, the set fell to an unflattering 36 mph at Kingsbog before touching 60 mph at Mossley. Compare that to what *55* had achieved with an 11-coach load only a few days earlier.

Tuesday 8 July

This was the end of my first runabout ticket of summer '69 and still no steam. In an effort to preserve diesels and ensure no steam-hauled passenger trains, the 17.49 ex-York Road (Whiteabbey, Jordanstown and Greenisland only) was reduced to one double- (driving cab) ended MPD-unit. Anchor car *65* formed the entire train! Making 51 mph out the Lough shore was hardly wonderful, but worse was to come! As previously explained, the MPD units only had one engine per car. So when that fails there is nothing to provide power. That is precisely what happened to *65*. It gurgled to a stop in Whiteabbey and then the driver spent 24 minutes trying to get the thing going again! Meanwhile, the boat train and boat passengers were held behind! I just had a good chuckle and reckoned that justice had been done. Had the shed supplied a steam train – even on the little 17.49 – this would not have happened.

Saturday 12 July

The next week or so would produce an abundance of steam-hauled trains – an abundance never to be repeated again. I was conscious of this and so was my younger brother, so I encouraged him to join me for the week. What a good decision that was and what great value we eked out of the runabout tickets, purchased at Lisburn that morning.

This is a particularly important day in Northern Ireland's calendar. Some may feel that infamous is a better term, but I use the word 'important' because it was the last 'Twelfth' when 'the men' were transported by a steam train. Not that the 'Twelfth' itself always provided a feast of steam – that tended to be reserved for the days immediately after, when lots of folks would go to the seaside, by train!

Let me explain a couple of background matters about this particular 'Twelfth'. Since the 'big day' fell on a Saturday, most businesses did not close up until the previous evening. So many people were catapulted into their two (or even three) week holiday by way of 'eleventh night' celebrations. This late stop for the traditional 'July fortnight' was one of the reasons for the recent scarcity of steam, for the previous week had had all the negatives – no schools, no colleges and very few trippers. Even for those not taking this particular fortnight off, 12 July is a bank holiday and 13 July a day on which most businesses (other than banks) remain shut. Since 12 July on this occasion was a Saturday and the 13 July a Sunday, this meant that banks would be shut on Monday 14 and most businesses on Tuesday 15. These two days in particular featured a host of the Portrush specials, as detailed in NIR's 'July Holiday Arrangements 1969', which was published prior to 11 July and was intended to be read in conjunction with the then current summer timetable.

Returning to the Twelfth, for steam enthusiasts the main venue of interest was that for the East Antrim lodges, at Larne. Since Belfast (and apparently Whiteabbey also) does not fall within this jurisdiction, it meant that excursion trains were worked empty to the first pick-up point, which on this occasion was Jordanstown. Two excursions were steam-hauled, while an edict had

been passed (if you could ever have any faith in such!) that the 07.55 and 14.05 boat trains would be steam on Saturdays for the rest of the summer. I did not drag myself out of bed early enough to check the 07.55 (I would do so on many occasions as the summer drew on), but NIR certainly honoured their word regarding the 14.05. So in total, three engines were involved in passenger trains that day – *50*, *53* and *55*. The first special was due away from Jordanstown at 10.21 and was nearly twenty minutes late arriving from York Road.

Paddy Dobbin driving *50*, hauling a mere snip of a load of ten coaches, worked as well as might be expected. But with stops at Greenisland and Carrickfergus to pick up more 'brethren' and slacks at Whitehead, Ballycarry and Magheramorne, speed never exceeded 47 mph. We detrained at Larne Town for the mere reason of taking the second excursion round to the Harbour. So we sampled a cameo appearance of Bertie Wright driving *55* (again with ten coaches) over the slow mile into the terminus. Both trains would remain at Larne Harbour until the end of

Engine 55 *on a return 'Orangeman's' special at Larne Town on 12 July 1969.*

General view of Larne Harbour layout on 12 July 1969. No 53 has arrived with the 14.05 from York Road. While not involved in passenger duties, 51 is on hand to assist with shunting.

the parade, so it was a case of getting back by diesel (three-car MED set with power cars *18* and *19*) on the 13.15 ex-Larne Harbour, as far as Greenisland. The 14.05 ex-York Road was also running late and involved engine *53* and the lightest load of the day – just eight coaches! Driver R Kemp of Larne was never a man to work an engine, though 51 mph before Carrickfergus, 48 mph round the curves before Whitehead and 45 mph between Ballycarry and Magheramorne were all better than the ten-coach struggle earlier that morning. Even so, long station work had also contributed to the nine-minute late departure from Greenisland becoming a deficit of 19 minutes by Larne Harbour.

Paddy Dobbin and *50* again took up the first homebound special, and most of the enthusiasts opted for this one because it would be possible to get back (at least as far as Carrickfergus) to cover the return boat train. The non-stop run to Carrickfergus was dull in the extreme, being delivered without exceeding 44 mph. However, Dobbin was not going to be embarrassed by the Mount bank, and after a steady 21 mph up the steepest part, he got *50* away to over 31 mph

before the stop at Greenisland. This, we had to admit, was better than some MPD sets achieved up that bank! There followed a long stop at Jordanstown, to allow Orangemen, bandsmen and their supporters to disembark, and 50 mph was eventually exceeded as the almost empty train strolled in along the lough shore.

A rather nasty incident occurred before boarding the diesel back to Carrickfergus. While standing in the main concourse of York Road station, a roughly spoken Glaswegian bandsman, clearly much the worse for drink, staggered over and accused me of uttering an expletive concerning Her Royal Majesty, the Queen. Now, I'm sure the said young chap has now had plenty of time to sober up, so let me assure him that, while I might not be the greatest supporter of 'loyalism' in Northern Ireland, my whole family could certainly be described as 'Royal' subjects! Joking aside, this was not a pleasant incident, and I have to be grateful to his mate, who was obviously not so intoxicated and quietly suggested that I had not been the purveyor of such a sentiment. So, raised arms were lowered, but just for a moment I had looked straight into the eye of

View at York Road after arrival of 53 with the 17.20 ex-Larne Harbour. No 51 is shunting vans in Platform 2.

a vicious combination of intolerance and bigotry mixed with a lethal dose of alcohol.

The best run of the day was reserved for last. With a large number of 'Twelfth' supporters still making their way back from Larne, the 17.05 boat train was switched to a diesel and *53*, with her eight-coach load now swollen by an additional van, was given the 17.20 stopping train. The passage of specials had left everything running hideously late, but we had been counting on this to make the 'double-back' to Carrickfergus. Driver Bobby Vance had *53* in great form and 37 mph through Trooperslane, with a train of this size, was good work. Extra stops were made at Jordanstown and Whiteabbey (with top speeds of 40 mph and 34 mph respectively) and then Vance made a spirited sprint in along the lough shore, with a maximum of 56 mph. My personal book of good runs on the Larne line, with loads of eight or more coaches, is a thin volume! But this is one of them.

Monday 14 July

The first steam train to Portrush was at 09.25 and we should have been on it. But on arrival at York Road, I recall there was a problem with Paul's runabout ticket and this necessitated myself returning to Great Victoria Street. (I wasn't going to ask a 12-year-old to 'hoof' the one and a half miles between the two stations three times in a morning.)

So we took the second 'special', which had Coleraine driver Jimmy Coulter provided with number *4* and a nine-coach load. A poor start out the lough shore and only 41 mph at Whitehouse was followed by an equally lax climb up the bank. There was no question of *4* being in any trouble – she just wasn't being worked hard enough and speed fell to 17 mph at Monkstown. The regulator setting for the uphill section was little changed for the downhill and we raced away to 66 mph at Dunadry and the first stop in Antrim. A similar pattern was repeated on to Ballymena, with speed only flickering above 40 mph on the climb to Post 26 and yet a respectable 60 mph was touched after Kellswater. More passengers taken on and a swift water stop completed, a fairly spirited start up through Cullybackey followed, with 36 mph before the hand tablet exchange and a steady 38–39 mph up to Post 38. We then had an

End of the line at Portrush on 14 July 1969. Driver Jimmy Coulter has a word with Mac Arnold while (from left to right) Norman Foster, Ian Wilson and Irwin Pryce look on.

A warm afternoon's siesta at Coleraine shed for (from left to right) 50, 4 and 53.

unscheduled stop at Killagan, but still attained 53 mph beforehand. A signal check at Ballyboyland gates ruined the run down to Ballymoney, with just 52 mph before and after the check. The section on to Coleraine was quite good and would have been even better but for the continuing A26 slack. Coulter was away to 57 mph at Post 58, which in the past would have been sufficient to provide a maximum well into the mid-60s down Windyhall housing estate. However, the occasion was deemed 'big enough' for Portstewart cabin to be 'switched in', so necessitating a hand tablet exchange. So a run of 12 minutes or thereabouts, with 36 mph before and 40 mph after the exchange, was not bad and we reached the seaside terminus just seven minutes late. Once again, the old adage of 'country drivers getting better the closer they get to home' rang true!

In all, three steam trains got to Portrush that morning with *50* and *53* the other engines involved. This double-act would completely dominate the Portrush scene for the next two weeks.

There was still a question over the 13.15 regular train. This was actually officially noted to be steam-hauled throughout the holiday period. Paul and I made our way back as far as Ballymoney and then awaited developments. When the 13.15 eventually appeared, York Road had provided a six-car MED set, ably driven by Percy Mitchell.

Now the MEDs (a bit like the 450-class) were very suitable for short journeys. They were equipped with automatic doors and low-back bus-type seats, which could actually be reversed to suit the direction of the train's motion. Since the doors were automatic, there was no need for windows that opened and ventilation was provided by top quarter windows, though these would often be stuck in permanently open or closed positions. It seems that the latter situation was predominant in the set provided on this day.

The morning weather had held much promise of a good day and the afternoon turned into a scorcher – one of those rare days in Northern Ireland when the temperature rises above 24^{0}C (75^{0}F). People who hadn't initially contemplated a day to the seaside, suddenly thought this might be a good idea. Add to this the fact that the promotional afternoon fare on the 13.15 was so cheap (at 7s 6d or 37.5p) that it was actually referred to in *Railway Magazine*. Not surprisingly then, a large number of people turned up to buy their afternoon 'returns' to Portrush, involving a long run in a hot box which reeked of diesel and whose windows wouldn't open! The 13.15 was due to cross the 12.30 ex-Londonderry at Cullybackey and I can confirm that the latter (a four-car MPD set with power units *64, 45* and *57*) was already running 25 minutes late at Ballymoney, where Paul and I had detrained. As shall be seen, the long delay at Cullybackey was a common feature of the 13.15 that summer. But for this troop of passengers it apparently came as a major relief. The story goes that Percy got out of the cramped cab and strolled down the platform to stretch his legs. An upright young fellow who exclaimed "My wife's on that train and she's pregnant", accosted him! Feigning moral indignation (rather than honouring his role as a public servant of NIR) at such an accusation, Percy retorted "That's not my fault!" Then the signalman (for there were no station staff at Cullybackey) arranged a bucket of water with some cups and provided some relief for people who, by now, were probably wishing they had stayed at home.

Certainly the eventual arrival of this train at Ballymoney resembled a tube train on the Piccadilly line at rush hour. Paul and I, not wishing to add to the discomfort factor, merely smiled and waved it on. By the next day the 13.15 would be in the capable 'hands' of not one, but two steam engines, and a good rake of airy steam coaches!

We made our way back to Coleraine on the 14.50 ex-York Road. Usually this would be a Hampshire turn, but was today reduced to a seven-car MPD set (including light refreshment car and 'steam' coach) and, in fine MPD-style, running over 20 minutes late! There hadn't been any rostered steam turns on the branch, but we did pick up an empty coaches run into Portrush, with Bertie Wright driving *53* and a ten-coach rake in easy style.

Bertie's run, however, was not as 'easy' as the next run to be described. The first steam special out of Portrush involved driver John Scott of Ballymena, with number *50* and a ten-coach load. Now, John Scott was a very easy man on the engines and we only got on this train because we were assured a 'double back' to Coleraine, where we would pick up a later special. So a few extra steam miles would be recorded – but quantity rather than quality! This night, for instance, with a signal stop at Portstewart, he actually managed to run the entire length of the Portrush branch without exceeding 30 mph! The section on to Ballymoney was reckless by comparison, with 45 mph after Macfin! Of course, this style of running told us absolutely nothing about *50*'s state of health, and that would be a matter of great importance over the next two weeks.

A six-car Hampshire set (power units *72* and *75*) whisked us back to Coleraine. Now, the good weather and the crowds of people were actually forcing NIR to despatch trains before their appointed times. They were obviously intending to mop up the entire procedure with a final late diesel turn. So *4*, with her nine-coach rake, aptly in the hands of Jackie Kitchen (driving) and Willie Graham (firing), left Coleraine nearly 12 minutes early. In many ways this combination is my best cameo of the holiday atmosphere of the return trip from Portrush – and it was a cameo which was to last for some time. Both Kitchen and Graham were young men and would be around the railway for many years to come, while number *4* ultimately became the preserved jeep and this fusion, of men and machine, would frequently be seen on the RPSI's 'Portrush Flyer' of the late 1970s and early 1980s. The run home embodied much of that flair, except that here it was real – not preserved.

A good start was made out of Coleraine and although the A26 bridge slack was religiously observed, we still managed two miles at a steady 54 mph after Macfin. After a shaky start out of Ballymoney, there was some tremendous 'stir' up

Ballyboyland, with bets made that the engine could be heard in Ballycastle! We went past Ballyboyland cabin at over 41 mph, before *4* showed the first signs of being a little winded and fell to 36 mph before Post 48. We were actually booked to stop at Dunloy, but with the earlier path that *4* and her crew were now tracing, this stop was omitted and we headed on to Cullybackey to cross the 20.00 ex-York Road. ('Omitted' indeed, for Kitchen took the hand tablet exchange at Dunloy at no less than 46 mph!) Nothing more than 55 mph was recorded at Glarryford, but the time of just over 25 minutes to stop in Cullybackey was good for a train of this size.

However, all the hard work was to little avail, for we sat for 12 minutes awaiting the diesel. In the time available we could easily have slipped on down the easy three miles to Ballymena, and I can only speculate that the real reason for the delay was that we had actually caught the special ahead. During the stop, Graham should have been attending to number *4*'s boiler. Instead, he was exhibiting his youthful physique to every young lady willing to give him a second glance! The result was that once we got the 'right away' he overfilled her boiler, thus subjecting *4* to a spot of priming. However, this was quickly remedied and a reasonable 50 mph was attained down the rock cutting before Ballymena.

Five minutes were spent taking water and pulling the train forward to ensure access from the rear coach. This was an additional nuisance feature with heavy stopping trains. A solid run on to Antrim was completed in just over 14 minutes, with 61 mph at Kellswater, 56 mph over Post 26 and 61 mph again after Cookstown Junction. But it was the last section on to York Road that held sheer entertainment value, even if it wasn't a classic run up the hill! Here was the formula: Kitchen would start working *4* for all she was worth and for a while all would go well; then the engine would start to flag under the strain and he'd have to ease her – very likely steam pressure was falling; Graham was also labouring away, so he would eventually recover the pressure, thus allowing Kitchen to open the engine up again.

This formula produced 44 mph at Muckamore, with 41 mph held over the steepest part of the bank at Dunadry, and away to a very creditable 47 mph after Templepatrick. Then the easing reduced speed to 39 mph at Doagh, where the engine was once again opened up, ensuring a steady 39–40 mph over the last two miles to the summit.

During 1967, NIR imposed various permanent way speed restrictions on the downhill section from Kingsbog. Until then, drivers could afford to be a bit lax on the uphill work, knowing that a last dash towards the lough shore, with speed rapidly rising into the low or mid 70s would claw back a few minutes of lost time. Even though some of those limits had been lifted, reliance on swift descents seemed to have faded permanently. At first it appeared that tonight's descent would fall into the pattern of most others described herein. The big train was away to 58 mph at Mossley when the first heavy brake application was made, reducing speed to 49 mph at Monkstown. Then Kitchen did something unusual. He did not make the now almost mandatory second application of the brakes over the viaduct (crossed at 62 mph) and so we accelerated towards Whitehouse, eventually touching 71 mph. So 4 became the first engine for more than three months to record a '70', but she would not be the last! This final sprint culminated in a very satisfactory time of 26 m 48 s in from Antrim and an arrival at York Road 'technically' more than a minute ahead of schedule.

There was time for only a few words of banter with other enthusiasts, because Paul and I still had to walk to Great Victoria Street, travelling back to Lisburn via the 22.45 local (three-car BUT set, with power units 123 and 135). From there we cycled home, arriving tired, but very satisfied just after a quarter past eleven. We didn't get much sleep either, for before 7.30 am we would both be up and ready to do it all again!

Tuesday 15 July

There were no ticket problems this morning, so we boarded the 09.25 special at York Road. York Road shed had obviously been satisfied with reports on the three engines from the previous day,

for the same combination was in play. Number 50 and Harry Ramsey, with an eight-coach load, formed this first excursion. The run to Antrim was bad and that on to Ballymena even worse! Number 50 could be fraught with steaming problems, while on other occasions she could be magic. This morning was one of the aforementioned occasions. We managed 45 mph at Whitehouse, fell to a very unflattering 17 mph at Monkstown and then just shaded 60 mph at Dunadry. Clearly all was not well, for after topping 40 mph at Post 26 and away to 48 mph at Post 27, Ramsey shut 50 off altogether and 'drifted' down to Kellswater. Large numbers of enthusiasts detrained at Ballymena!

However, 53 and Lawrence McCahon on the 10.20 special were not much better. With a nine-coach rake, running was dull in the extreme. Weak uphill work and nothing more than 52 mph before the Dunloy hand tablet exchange and again before a gate check, identical to that of the previous day, ruined any chance of speed down Ballyboyland.

That morning, just two specials were steam. NIR were not about to repeat the mistakes of the day before, and so a ten-coach steam train was rostered for the 13.15 ex-York Road. Number 4 was the choice of train engine, but the shed also provided a pilot engine to Antrim – number 55! It is interesting to note the hierarchy that had developed. Numbers 4, 50 and 53 were the preferred engines for main-line workings – both in view of their perceived mechanical order and their high-bunk, which allowed for greater mileage before refuelling. Numbers 51 and 55 also had high bunks, but 55 was now the only other choice for mainline steam.

Paul and I returned from Ballymoney courtesy of the six-car MPD set (power units 38, 42, 53 and 60) forming the 10.45 ex-Londonderry. Despite having four power units we still fell to 37 mph before Kingsbog, which places in context the uphill work of the heavily laden steam trains. With the lost time, we had just a little concern about making the connection at York Road. Eventually the diesel trundled into Platform 3 just over two minutes before the steam train's advertised

Some evidence of a dirty fire as 50 starts out of Ballymena with the 09:25 to Portrush on 15 July 1969.

departure time. Sitting at Platform 2 was the long 13.15, with *55* at the head and *4* next. It is interesting to reflect on and compare and contrast the combination. Here, for me, was the best of the single numbers (*10* was effectively regarded as a 'single numbered' engine) and the best of the *50*s. Number *4* pointed chimney first, while *55* was orientated bunk-first, so they were coupled chimney to chimney. One engine was totally steeped in NCC history – the other had spent many years on the Great Northern. One engine would be preserved – the other would not. Both engines would share a very different platform, in more subdued circumstances, within a month. One engine was today making her last appearance in Portrush under a 'company' banner – the other had already taken her last bow at the seaside town.

The driver on the train engine, Rab Graham, would become the hero of many enthusiasts, new and old, that summer. Here was a man so willing to share in the last days of passenger steam in Northern Ireland, that he actually changed turns with another driver to ensure his presence in the cab during the following week.

We were away nearly four minutes late, but had little difficulty in recouping this before Ballymena. A speed of 27–28 mph sustained over Mossley followed 52 mph at Whitehouse. The jeeps were quite capable of speeds into the low-80s, but only when in chimney-first orientation. (Bunk-first operations seldom netted anything much above 70 mph.) So once we were away to 60 mph at Doagh, the engines were eased and a maximum of 68 mph attained through Dunadry. We stopped just short of Antrim station in just 26 m 29 s from York Road. Number *55* ran forward, crossing to the 'up' road, and then *4* moved ahead into the station. On to Ballymena, Graham provided a fair run, considering the load, with 45 mph up to Post 26, 58 mph at Kellswater and a time of 16 m 24 s from Antrim. We took water and then made an easy run up to Cullybackey (maximum 35 mph) where we were due to cross the 12.30 ex-Londonderry. Long stops at Cullybackey, due to late running of the diesel, became a feature of this train. Such was the case

Jeep 50 passing Dhu Varren with the 18.40 branch train to Coleraine on 15 July 1969.

Back to Portrush again and 50 collects the additional four coaches from Platform 1.

today, so while we await the 'offender' I shall digress a little.

The weather is still warm – not quite as warm as Monday, but close enough. Paul and I have been travelling pretty constantly that day. Further on down the coach, some young ladies have their transistor radios ('trannies' to them!) playing. The songs wafting up to our ears include the 'Stones' biggest latter-day hit 'Honky Tonk Woman', but even more emphatic on the play-list is a mega-hit by unknown group Thunderclap Newman, called 'Something in the Air'. Like it or loathe it you cannot escape this one!

We're thirsty. The signalman says the diesel won't be in for another ten minutes; so there is enough time to 'race down' the village's main street to the general store and buy a bottle of something that this particular part of County Antrim is famous for – lemonade – or if we're feeling adventurous, perhaps a bottle of lemon and limeade!

Some years later I was working as a laboratory assistant in the Agriculture Department of Queen's University. The particular job performed that day was not a pleasant one, for it involved milling grass samples which would then undergo the chemical process of digestion. It's hot and it's dusty and I have my radio playing in the background. The disc jockey announces an 'oldie'. 'Something in the Air' starts to play and all of a sudden I remember that I'm really very thirsty!

Back to the story, and a steady start up to Post 38 was followed by a maximum of 57 mph before Dunloy, where the hand tablet exchange was taken at a respectable 42 mph. Graham was preparing to give us a good run down Ballyboyland (59 mph before Post 50) when, for the third time in two days, we were severely checked by the level crossing gates not being open in time. After Ballymoney we touched 56 mph before the bridge slack. Being a regular train, the 13.15 was subject to request stops at University, Cromore (Portstewart renamed!) and Dhu Varren. This day we made one at Dhu Varren, so the time of 10 m 40 s from Coleraine

(maximum 41 mph) probably represented some sort of a record – for just a little while!

In the early evening, one branch local was steam-hauled. This involved *50*, with a six-coach load, on an 18.40 to Coleraine only (see opposite and page 99). Paddy Dobbin managed 32 mph at Post 66 and 46 mph at the University, after a rather slow hand tablet exchange at Portstewart, and cut the 15-minute branch schedule by nearly two minutes The return journey was technically an 'empty coaches' working, with nothing more than 38 mph and two minutes again lopped off the schedule.

Four more coaches had been added to *50*'s rake before getting away with the 19.45 special to York Road. This run started well, with Paddy mounting Post 66 at 30 mph and then doing 46 mph at the University. A speed of 51 mph before Ballymoney was alright, but the run up Ballyboyland was poor, with only 31 mph at the cabin and a momentary minimum of 29 mph thereafter. Even though speed exceeded 55 mph round Dunminning, this was turning into a very dull affair and so we got off at Ballymena. Engine *50*'s morning steaming problems seemed to have persisted.

The 20.10 return excursion was in the hands of Bertie Wright and *53*. Bertie was up to his 'clever runs with ten coaches' approach, described earlier. Speed was accelerating towards 55 mph when we encountered a signal check at Kellswater – just the worst place, for we then dragged up to Post 26 at 40–42 mph and did nothing more than 51 mph before Antrim. Then the work started, for we were still doing over 50 mph before Dunadry. Speed went down to 43 mph over the steepest part, but Wright recovered to over 45 mph after Templepatrick. Speed did just dip below the 'bell-wether' '40' over the last mile to the summit (minimum 38 mph) – but this still bettered the morning's 'express' diesel! We were away to 54 mph at Post 10 when furious braking brought us to a momentary stop at Monkstown – to allow an employee off. There was little need for any further caution, so Wright got the big train away swiftly and touched 62 mph at Whitehouse. So it was into

No 50 making a fairly lacklustre start out of Ballymena with the 19.45 special ex-Portrush on 15 July 1969.

York Road even later that the previous evening and home to bed for a good night's sleep, for, with the two-day holiday over, only the regular 13.15 was rostered steam for the morrow.

Wednesday 16 July

Paul and I got off the 12.15 ex-Lisburn at Great Victoria Street and made our way along York Street, past Gallaher's tobacco factory. Gallaher's did not officially close for the whole of the July fortnight and some of the operatives were sitting along York Street, enjoying their packed lunches in the warm sunshine. I walked on, unaware that I would end up working for this establishment for nearly 20 years, and would become very tuned into their working practices. Mac Arnold met us with the interesting information that, with the continuing good weather, an additional excursion train had been required that morning, and so *53* had already been despatched to Portrush. Typical – just when you relaxed and had a bit of a sleep in, you were caught off guard! A steam run to Coleraine was missed because we had believed NIR would do what they said they were going to do! Strangely enough, for over the past two days she seemed to

have produced the best of the runs, *4* had been despatched to the Great Northern on the 'ballast' train. That left 'bad-steaming' *50* as first choice for the 13.15, but the nine-coach train was also given a pilot in the form of *55* to Kingsbog. It was Rab Graham's day off, so Jackie Kitchen was in charge of *50*, while Jimmy Simpson was having one of his 'steam engines are great' days on *55*. Unfortunately, there was a permanent way restriction in force at the very worst place – on the country bound side of the Bleach Green Viaduct. We roared away to 56 mph at Whitehouse, went through Whiteabbey (in 6 m 54 s from York Road) still doing 50 mph and then braked to 21 mph for the restriction. Then we accelerated steadily up the bank, recovering to 34 mph at Monkstown, 35 mph at Mossley and 39 mph at Ballyclare Junction. A direct comparison with Wright and Kitchen's run with *4/5* on 10 May shows a very similar pattern – except that *50/55* are generally about one mph better throughout. So we can estimate that the two engines would have held about 38 mph had the restriction not been in place.

I've said it before, but at this stage it is worth repeating – *50* was just the most temperamental machine imaginable! One day she was in foul

No 55's sole duty on 16 July 1969 was to pilot the 13.15 to Kingsbog Junction – but what a duty! Jimmy Simpson nods farewell to Jackie Kitchen on 50 and heads back to York Road.

form, the next day sparkling. She could even be lousy for part of a journey and then much improved for the rest. You just never knew. Today she was sparkling. Devoid of *55's* assistance, Kitchen ran the ten miles down to Antrim in 11 m 34 s, touching 75 mph at Dunadry and producing the biggest steam speed of 1969. At this stage we were running early, but he continued to Ballymena with a fine time of 14 m 46 s, with a steady 47 mph through Cookstown Junction and 63 mph at Kellswater. We were severely checked by signals on the section up to Cullybackey, but fortunately this was because the diesel was imminent. So we were away for Ballymoney only two minutes behind schedule, with 60 mph before Dunloy, where the hand tablet was taken at 42 mph, and then a fine 68 mph down Ballyboyland. Even so, we still lost almost two minutes on the impossible 20-minute schedule. We reached 59 mph before Macfin and then the A26 bridge slack took its toll. We were just over five minutes late into Coleraine, but foreman, big Ernie Sinclair, was not going to keep us too long, and after some efficient station work we were away on the final section to Portrush. To arrive on time Kitchen and *50* needed

to pick up four minutes on the branch. They did precisely that, with speed rising to 48 mph at Post 66 and a very fine time in from Coleraine of 10 m 59 s.

After a bit of sunbathing (yes Portrush was actually warm enough on occasions that summer to permit such activities!), it was back to the station. Steam was now required on the 17.05 branch train to Coleraine. This was also the means to get *50* to Coleraine for turning – so both branch locals were in 'bunk-first' mode, not that that particularly mattered. John Scott appeared and, although the load had been reduced to a modest and very workable four coaches, he managed to take nearly 22 minutes to reach Coleraine, including stops at all three intermediate stations and a top speed of just 34 mph! On the 18.35 return working he took just 19 minutes, including the three stops. "Good run?" I chided fellow-timer Irwin Pryce on our return to Portrush. "Well" said Irwin thoughtfully, and without recourse to expletives, "a run!"

Apparently Scott was running so far behind time on the return trip out of Portrush, that the train had to be stopped at Kingsbog, where he

No 50 on the 13.15 ex-York Road awaits an MPD-set on the 12.45 ex-Londonderry at Cullybackey on 16 July 1969.

Not much 'stour' as 50 starts out of University with the 17.05 branch train to Coleraine on 16 July 1969.

swapped turns with the driver on the 22.00 ex-York Road. This ensured that he got home to Ballymena that night!

Meanwhile, most of us left Portrush on the 19.45 (extra) with *53*, eight coaches and Bertie Wright driving. With a lighter load than on the previous evening, we anticipated a better run – but we were generally disappointed. He managed 44 mph on the branch and was through Coleraine in thirteen minutes, but then failed to exceed 50 mph after Macfin. The run up Ballyboyland was solid, with a steady 38–39 mph all the way up. Then we did nothing more than 53 mph at Glarryford, and the time of 31 m 48 s from Ballymoney to Ballymena was disappointing. The section on to Belfast was dull too, with 56 mph at Kellswater, 48 mph at Post 26 and just 53 mph before Antrim. He tried to run up the hill, but was generally below the previous night's effort, falling to below 38 mph at Kingsbog. With no forced stop at Monkstown, no '60' on the lough shore either (maximum 55 mph) and a final time from Ballymena of 41 m 42 s, it was an instantly forgettable journey – though obviously better than the ordeal John Scott's passengers were having to suffer! Poor *53* was about to be plagued by one problem after another and I wonder if that night, we were just starting to see the first effects of worn piston rings. By Saturday she would be in a miserable condition.

Thursday 17 July

There were no extras today and no pilot either! Rab Graham was back to work with *50* and a nine-coach load. We just exceeded 45 mph out the lough shore, but *50* was soon a bit winded and fell to 16 mph after Monkstown, before Graham got her pulled round and got away to 66 mph at Dunadry. Now there was an elderly lady who lived in the neighbourhood of Drumsough and once a week she had a day out to Portrush. When this occurred, the train would make a special stop at Cookstown Junction. Even with the stop, the schedule of 18 minutes from Antrim to Ballymena was kept. A respectable 45 mph was achieved before the stop, with 58 mph at

Kellswater afterwards. Engine *50* was definitely in more rebellious form and gave trouble on the restart from Ballymena. Once away, we did at least manage 36 mph before Cullybackey where, for once, the diesel was actually waiting! This was followed by just 54 mph before Dunloy and a more leisurely hand exchange (at 35 mph). Then we touched 60 mph before Post 50, when another infernal gate slack compounded to give a time of 23 m 45 s from Cullybackey. So it was on to Coleraine and we managed 58 mph before the bridge slack. However, the best piece of running of the day was on the branch, when the section from Coleraine to stop in Dhu Varren was completed in just 9 m 51 s, with 47 mph after Portstewart.

This evening the 19.00 branch train to Coleraine was steam-hauled. For some unknown reason the load was only reduced to seven coaches. Graham was reasonably sharp in both directions with 48 mph on the outward journey and 43 mph on the inbound. However, late running of the 18.00 ex-York Road ensured an arrival at Portrush little more than a minute before the 19.55 departure time – and three coaches still had to be added. Shunting, adding coaches and allowing the passengers to fill them took over fifteen minutes, so it was almost 20.10 before we departed. Once again, being a normal scheduled train, we were subject to discretionary stops at the intermediate stations on the branch. With a load of ten coaches, this was no easy assignment. Graham stopped in Dhu Varren in well under the time many a driver would have taken to pass. Then, starting up the 1/76 at Post 67 he actually managed 30 mph at Post 66, before a Cromore (Portstewart) stop. Anyone viewing us from the caravan sites, that straddle the railway above Dhu Varren, would certainly have beheld the fine sight of a steam train being worked at full stretch. The section on to Coleraine was run in less than seven minutes, with a very satisfactory maximum of 49 mph through University. Then it was 53 mph after Macfin and a time of 13 m 34 s to stop in Ballymoney – a reasonable performance. The start up Ballyboyland was good, with 37 mph just exceeded at the cabin, a minimum of 34 mph and then just 38 mph before an unscheduled Dunloy stop. Once again, further time was being lost because the long train had to be pulled up at virtually every stop.

More smart work followed on to Cullybackey (reached in 13 m 59 s from Dunloy), with 55 mph round Dunminning and 49 mph on the section into Ballymena. Poor Graham had done everything possible but, particularly with all the additional station time, we were now almost 32 minutes late. After a blistering start out to Kellswater, we actually made 60 mph with a ten-coach load (for just the second time that year). A minimum of 54 mph over Milepost 26, followed by an easy run down through Cookstown Junction (maximum 57 mph), netted a 14½ minute time to Antrim. There was plenty more bustle and activity up the bank, with 47 mph at Dunadry, 43 mph over the steepest point and 46 mph after Templepatrick. Poor old *50* had taken a lot of hard work and by Post 15 she was just a bit winded, with speed eventually falling to 35 mph at Kingsbog. We ran down the hill with a maximum of just 59 mph before Monkstown, but the fine start out of Antrim had been good enough to provide a very respectable 28 m 12 s in the terminus, with the clock showing 22:10 (exactly half-an-hour late).

While I had been enjoying the delights of mainline steam, the Larne line had not exactly given up on such a prospect. Consequently the 17:30 business express to Larne was steam on several evenings during this and subsequent weeks. Tonight driver Alan Robinson and *53* had provided some entertainment, for on arrival of the 19:15 return at Carrickfergus a problem was discovered with the engine's valve-motion. Fortunately enthusiast Derek Henderson (a ship's mechanic by trade) was on hand and was able to assist in putting the problem right. Alan Robinson duly obliged by running up to Greenisland in a manner that would not be out of place were we observing today's six-car 80-class rather than a six-coach steam train. Of course a six-car 80-class incorporates two power units. So much for NIR's claim that one 70-class unit (same power rating as the 80-class) equals one steam engine!

Carrickfergus, with the 19.15 ex-Larne Harbour. Derek Henderson, Alan Robinson and Peter Scott repair 53's motion.

Friday 18 July

On Thursday, *50* had been a well-behaved engine. On Friday she was in brilliant form! We had an eight-coach load and were just a couple of minutes late away. The run to Antrim was classic stuff for eight coaches – 48 mph at Whitehouse, a minimum of 24 mph at Mossley and 72 mph at Dunadry, with Antrim reached in 29 m 15 s from York Road. The old lady from Drumsough must have been getting plenty of value in Portrush, for we again made the Cookstown Junction stop, though not before 46 mph had been exceeded. So it was on to Ballymena, with 62 mph at Kellswater also very creditable. We ran up to Cullybackey (maximum 35 mph), where again the diesel was on time. Then it was on to Dunloy and *50* seemed to have gone 'a bit off the boil', for nothing more than 54 mph was recorded and then signals brought us to a complete standstill just short of the level crossing. That seemed to motivate us, for Graham then ran the seven and a half miles from the Dunloy outer home signal to Ballymoney in one second under the even ten minutes, with a maximum of 67 mph down

Ballyboyland. We managed 58 mph before the A26 bridge slack, reaching Coleraine in 12 m 14 s from Ballymoney, some five minutes late. A Dhu Varren stop was inserted and yet we still reached Portrush on time, courtesy of a very sharp time of 9 m 21 s from Coleraine to Dhu Varren and a maximum speed of 48 mph.

On Fridays only, the 17.20 commuter train to Cullybackey was strengthened (in terms of length rather than reliable motive power) and also extended to Portrush. This train then formed the 19.55, so the 13.15 returned in an earlier path – the 17.50 ex-Portrush. Maybe it was just as well that we had an earlier departure, for just before the run home the good weather had broken and it had started to rain. This seemed to dampen the ardour of my old schoolmate, Philip Preece. Having just purchased a runabout ticket, he was having second thoughts on whether he would make full use of it, and had practically put it up for auction! (Philip – you don't know what you gave up!) My current ticket ran out on this very evening, and there was certainly the promise of at least another week of steam on the 13:15 (if you

The station clock says it all as 50 makes an on-time arrival at Portrush on 18 July 1969 despite diesel hold-ups at (and diesel timings after) Cullybackey.

could believe the circulars). So I 'made him an offer he couldn't refuse' and purchased the rest of his ticket. And that is how, for NIR purposes only, I became 'Philip Preece' for the period between 19 July and 24 July 1969!

The run home was actually deemed good enough to be featured in RM Arnold's *NCC Saga* (in particular refer to the Appendix) and I don't wish to repeat what is written there. But it is worth putting the run in the context of what had been happening all week. We were just over three minutes late away and Graham made a very solid start, with 31 mph at Post 66 and 50 mph through the University, before a bad signal check added about a minute and a half to the journey time to Coleraine. The section on to Ballymoney was nothing special, with just 52 mph after Macfin and the run up Ballyboyland again demonstrated the more 'winded' side of *50*. After a good start and nearly 40 mph at the cabin, we fell to 33 mph at Post 49, but then *50* recovered to 43 mph before the Dunloy hand tablet exchange. The run then steadily improved, with the first 60 mph by a steam train round Dunminning in what seemed like an eternity and 62 mph before the stop in Cullybackey. Here we crossed the 18.10 ex-York Road, which was running slightly late. The trouble was that we were now six minutes late, and the diesel schedule didn't allow for our three and a bit minute stop at Ballymena to take water. So, even after another 50 mph down the rock cutting into Ballymena, our deficit had grown to nine minutes. We took just six minutes to pass Kellswater, doing 64 mph, fell to 57 mph at Post 26 and then touched 65 mph before the stop in Antrim, reached in 13 m 41 s and a minute clawed back. But it was the final section where we got the run of the year. Graham had *50* roaring away at 51 mph to Dunadry, held 48 mph over the worst part and continued to accelerate to 52 mph at Templepatrick. Speed then dropped off toward the summit, but we still went past Kingsbog at 45 mph. We didn't brake at Monkstown and approached the Bleach Green viaduct at 69 mph. Then and only then were the brakes applied, reducing speed along the lough shore to the high 50s. Even so, we stopped at Platform 3 just three minutes behind time, with the station staff shaking their heads in disbelief and saying "The diesel doesn't usually run in this close to time!"

With the earlier arrival there was time to assemble in a circular group in the concourse of York Road station, where the older enthusiasts would tell tales of trains long gone and of drivers and engines that I was born too late to know. But one thing that I was not too late to do, was to record these last events and the final countdown was to start tomorrow.

Saturday 19 July

We hadn't seen much of *51* that summer, though she had made it to Portrush on three occasions during the Sunday School season. But today she was York Road's choice for the two steam boat trains, which were well patronised and required eight coaches. John Weatherup of Larne took the driving honours on both trains, and that led to some similarity in the running. The 07.55 was almost five minutes late away from York Road and was dull out to Greenisland, with just 44 mph before and 34 mph after the Whiteabbey stop. Then Weatherup astounded us all with a breath-taking descent through the Mount (at 59 mph) and a stop into Carrickfergus so characteristic of Dan McAtamney that my logbook has his name crossed out! (Dan had brought the engine down from the shed that morning and then changed footplates with John Weatherup, thus compounding my confusion.) The time for the three miles from Greenisland was a remarkable 4 m 36 s! Round the Whitehead curves we touched 50 mph, with an eight-minute timing. Given the load, 42 mph before Ballycarry, 44 mph before Magheramorne, 43 mph before the Glynn stop and 39 mph before Larne was reasonable work and our arrival at the Harbour Station was just ten minutes late.

The homebound 09.40 was booked to run non-stop to York Road. The boat, as ever, was late and delayed our departure for half an hour. (Part of the logic in making the Saturday boat trains steam-hauled was to prevent a precious diesel

Maybe this explains the confusion in my log book! Driver McAtamney hands 51 over to driver Weatherup for the 07.55 to Larne Harbour on 19 July 1969.

sitting at Larne Harbour doing nothing for half the day!) We got an unchecked run as far as Carrickfergus, but between the hand tablet exchanges at Magheramorne and Ballycarry, the best we could manage was 47 mph on the single line and just over 50 mph at Downshire. We held a rather gloomy 33–34 mph through the Mount and got away to 45 mph at Post 6, when a series of signal checks ruined any decent progress into the city. This was a frequent problem with boat trains – if you lost your scheduled path you might well be further delayed behind a local train which had been despatched on time. We had taken nearly 43 minutes in from Larne Harbour (against the schedule of 35) – even if we had been unchecked, the time would still have been around 39 minutes.

The 14.05 was a little livelier, despite the addition of a four-wheeled van. We managed 45 mph at Whitehouse and produced another fast run through the Mount (this time just 58 mph recorded). Another eight minute, with a maximum speed of 50 mph, run to Whitehead followed. We

shaded 45 mph before the Ballycarry stop and 46 mph before the Magheramorne stop, and eventually reached Larne Harbour with the same time deficit as in the morning. This was not a bad finale for *51*. She would be back on the boat trains on the Saturday following, when the running would be even duller. But I would only observe her from afar on that occasion, so this was my farewell to this particular engine. I headed back to the city on the diesel that was leaving immediately (six-car MPD set, with power-units *40*, *52* and *64*). Running was so bad that the connection at 16.00 on to Portrush had to be delayed. This task was given to a three-car MED set, with cars *18* and *19*.

The hasty return to Portrush was because a steam special had unexpectedly gone there in the morning. I can't describe this as a Sunday School excursion (we defined that season as being from the second Saturday in May until the last Saturday in June), but in terms of the working it was very similar to the Doagh special that Harry Ramsey had been in charge of on 14 June. Harry was again in attendance, but while previously he had had *50* in good form, tonight he had a very sick *53*. The trouble was that her piston rings were badly worn on one side. She was shunting around Portrush, with such a big feeble blast coming from her chimney that one wondered if she could get herself up the 1/76 to Dhu Varren, never mind the ten-coach load she was expected to haul! Mac Arnold was on hand to offer Harry a few words of encouragement – he certainly needed them! We took nearly 16 minutes to clear Coleraine (only doing 20 mph at Post 66 and 45 mph through University) and didn't exceed 45 mph before Ballymoney. The best that can be said about the run up Ballyboyland was that, despite *53*'s obvious weakness, it was no worse than the usual sort of stuff Harry would provide. After a minimum of 26 mph at Post 52 we recovered to just over 31 mph, before falling back to less than 26 mph again at Post 49. The tablet was dropped at Dunloy, necessitating a stop and loss of a further three minutes. Then it was on to Ballymena and we actually did touch 53 mph round Dunminning. So far the run had been similar to that with the same engine on 17 May. Harry started out to Kellswater full of intent, but the weakness was again apparent and we only momentarily exceeded 53 mph. From there to hold 48 mph over Post 26 wasn't bad and we did actually exceed 61 mph before Antrim. Harry's plan was to get as much of a run at the bank as possible, for there was no doubt that *53* would fall back steadily. Then disaster struck! Someone attempted to open a carriage door at Antrim and the brakes were quickly applied. We were waved on, but speed was already down to 21 mph and poor *53* was in no state to recover quickly. With only 37 mph at Dunadry, we fell to 28 mph at what is now the Airport Road crossing, and only recovered to 33 mph at Templepatrick. What a difference when you consider *50*'s fine run five weeks earlier. We made a struggling start to Kingsbog with the almost empty train. Thereafter we did get 56 mph at Whitehouse – but reached York Road with some concern about the state of motive power for the following week.

Sunday 20 July

Paul and I were back on the Bangor line. My grandfather, who over the past six years had suffered a series of strokes had, in the past two weeks, deteriorated to the point that necessitated him being moved permanently to the geriatric hospital at Crawfordsburn. This was a hospital in whose grounds NIR had conveniently sited a halt. The 14.20 ex-Queen's Quay was in the hands of four-car MED set. Cars *26* and *27* were distinctly livelier than *28* and *29* had been two weeks beforehand, and managed over 51 mph between Sydenham and Holywood. The 14.20 wasn't booked to stop at Crawfordsburn but NIR, on hearing that Paul and I were going to visit our old sick grandfather, slotted an extra one in. Don't say they never had any compassion!

While we were visiting in hospital, three Americans were travelling a little further afield. Currently, they were within spitting distance of the moon! The papers had been full of expectation of history being made, which perhaps helped to explain why the same journalists had been slow to pick up on one of the year's more infamous stories. Although the incident was already two days old, it really only made 'page two' coverage today. This was the drowning of Mary Jo Kopechne in the car of Senator Edward Kennedy. Talk about convenient dates – and you think our politicians are good at timing, sound bites and spin these days!

Monday 21 July

A contrast of technology! The day that man landed on the moon, the afternoon train from Belfast to Portrush was steam-hauled. All morning long our eyes had been glued to the TV set – history in the making – "one small step for man, one giant leap for mankind". I have to confess to being mildly 'moon sceptic' at the time, for I felt that the millions of pounds invested could have been better utilised in a more humane way. I have to admit to a change of view since then. The technical work involved in getting the three men to the moon undoubtedly brought forward the computer revolution that has changed so many mundane jobs and generally improved the standard of living of everybody. It's a salutatory thought, but the machine assisting me to write this script could land an army of *Apollo XIs* on the moon!

Rab Graham had to struggle with some older technology. Yet again, *50* was York Road's choice on the 13.15 and the load was unchanged at eight coaches. Graham made an excellent start out the lough shore, exceeding 51 mph at Whitehouse. Then we slipped to 20 mph at Mossley, but a reasonable 65 mph at Dunadry took us into Antrim in exactly the half hour. Then there was another Cookstown Junction stop, with 44 mph before and 57 mph at Kellswater. We took water and had no trouble getting away up the rock cutting out of Ballymena and just exceeded 35 mph before running into Cullybackey almost to time. The 12.30 ex-Londonderry diesel was in dire form, so plenty of time for lemonade today! We were 20 minutes late leaving Cullybackey. Graham managed 57 mph before the hand tablet exchange at Dunloy and had just got away to 62 mph at Post 49 when a signal check, at Ballyboyland, alerted him to the fact that some members of the permanent way staff needed picked up. All these delays seemed to rile Graham, for he ran from Ballymoney to Coleraine in eleven minutes – despite observing the A26 slack. This involved doing over 60 mph before and an amazing 56 mph after the slack. Even better was the work over the Portrush branch, with 50 mph at Post 66 and four and a half minutes recovered to leave us just 19 minutes late into the terminus.

Now *50* probably worked some empty coaches back to Coleraine, where she would be turned and there would be a change of driver. I can only suggest that the guard on the 'empty coaches' was uncooperative, for I only have a record of returning to Coleraine on the 17.05 branch train in the hands of a four car MPD-set (power-units *46* and *59*). Steam (with populated coaches) was required on the 18.35 local ex-Coleraine, and by this time Tom Smith was on *50*'s footplate. For this the load had been reduced to just five coaches. A minute was gained over the branch despite a stop at the University and a further signal stop beyond Dhu Varren. A respectable maximum of 44 mph was attained. The same combination then worked the 19.00 local back to Coleraine. This was a lively little run, with over 38 mph at Post 66, 46 mph after Portstewart and a time of 11 m 49 s to Coleraine, despite the almost obligatory signal check at Post 62. We were certainly getting value today, for the 19.25 ex-Coleraine was also steam, with two minutes gained on the branch schedule (of 15), despite a further stop at the University. A maximum speed of 43 mph was reached at Post 66. This was the last occasion that I ever experienced steam on the Portrush branch locals and it was a fitting finale to what was always a very pleasant pastime, between the 'big run up and the big run back'.

Once again, shunting and marshalling the train, now restored to eight coaches, left us 17 minutes late out of Portrush. Smith's start out of Portrush was one of the best of the year, with over 35 mph at Post 66 and 46 mph after Portstewart. As earlier in the day, a signal check ruined the final approach to Coleraine. We then religiously observed the A26 slack and just touched 50 mph before Ballymoney. The run up Ballyboyland was very good – 40 mph at the cabin and nothing below 37 mph the rest of the way up. Once again Smith eased the engine for the easier undulating section and just managed 52 mph before Cullybackey. We trundled on down to Ballymena and took water. Thereafter we touched 60 mph 'on the race track' out to Kellswater. I think this stretch of line was NIR's first section of continuously welded rail and obviously provided the advantage of a comfortable run for both engine and crew. We held 53 mph up to Post 26, where the engine was shut off and allowed to drift down to the Antrim stop. We made a grand start out of Antrim, with over 47 mph at Dunadry, 42 mph at the Airport Road and away to over 47 mph again after Templepatrick. Then *50* faded a little and we eventually fell to just below 39 mph at Kingsbog. Thereafter we did no more than 55 mph at Mossley and were further impaired by a signal stop just outside the terminus. This was not quite to the moon and back, but I think I'd be happy with such an outing any day!

Tuesday 22 July

Auntie Mae had not had a holiday for some time, so she and a friend had gone off on a coach tour round Ireland. Before doing so, she had suggested that the family might like to use her house in Bangor. This would make it much easier to visit my grandfather, and we had taken up her kind offer. So when I left Lisburn shortly after midday, it was not to return. During the afternoon my mother and father and Paul made the car journey to Bangor. Later, I would make my way to Queen's Quay for the train to Bangor.

It was a replica of the previous day – same driver, same engine, same load! Graham made a very good start out to Seaview, with over 50 mph at Whitehouse. A better climb of the bank than on Monday, with a minimum of just under 22 mph at Mossley, allowed for easy running down the hill (maximum 62 mph) and still a very credible time

of 29 m 21 s to stop in Antrim. We were now on time and didn't have an extra stop at Cookstown Junction. So even after a relatively easy 43–44 mph climb to Post 26 and nothing more than 58 mph at Kellswater, we still ran into Ballymena nearly two minutes early (reached in just over 16 minutes from Antrim). We took water and headed for Cullybackey and were halted by signals just outside the village station. The diesel was only five minutes late, so there was no time to pick up a bottle! Since Kingsbog, *50* just seemed to be 'a bit off the boil'. Graham did his best to hold time on the next section, but with only 53 mph before Dunloy there was never a chance, even if he did take the hand tablet exchange at an incredible 46 mph (and there is more of this to come)! Even after a 65 mph dash down Ballyboyland, we had still dropped over two minutes on the tough schedule (of 20) to Ballymoney. On the section to Coleraine, *50* was worked to the very last possible moment, with the result that 62 mph was recorded before sharp braking for the A26 slack. We also got another 11-minute run over the Portrush branch – with 46 mph exceeded at Post

Across the lines: 50 *leaving Coleraine for Portrush with the 13.15 ex-York Road on 22 July 1969. This view is from the old harbour branch, with the mainline to Londonderry in the centre left.*

66 – to bring us into the seaside terminus just five minutes behind schedule.

NIR had provided 'double-ended' MPD-unit *65* for branch working and so, after taking *50* 'light engine' back to Coleraine for turning and watering, big Graham had to amuse himself by driving the equivalent of a bus up and down the branch!

With no local steam workings, the rostered train for the 19.55 did at least stand a chance of leaving close to time. So we were just four minutes late away, Graham and *50* cutting this deficit by over two minutes by Coleraine, with a good run on the branch – over 32 mph at Post 66 and 53 mph before University. The section on to Ballymoney was run tightly too, with 54 mph after Macfin and a time of under 13 minutes, despite the slack. However, when the challenging uphill section was encountered, *50*'s 'steam-shyness' reappeared. We gradually reached 35 mph at Ballyboyland cabin, but fell back to below 31 mph at Post 48 and then did no more than 54 mph round Dunminning. At only 46 mph between Cullybackey and Ballymena, and Graham was clearly taking every opportunity not to work *50*. After taking water, and now running 11 minutes late, we made a moderate start to Kellswater with 60 mph, but then fell to 52 mph at Post 26 and, in the style of the previous evening, shut off steam and drifted down to the Antrim stop. Another minute was lost where one might have been gained. Poor old *50* had gradually deteriorated all day. The best we could manage after Antrim was 44 mph at Dunadry. Once we had fallen to 37 mph at Post 17, *50* just hadn't enough steam to recover more than a couple of miles per hour and we eventually fell to a dismal 28 mph at Kingsbog. With the worst climb of the year, it was hard to reconcile the engine of Tuesday with that of the previous Friday. We free-wheeled down the hill, eventually touching 59 mph at Mossley. A bad signal just outside the terminus merely added to the gloom and we reached our destination over 14 minutes late, on an evening that had promised much.

We were all a bit despondent after this – it was a bit like seeing your favourite football team beaten 2–0 by a side that you felt they should have thrashed! I hadn't much time to hang around York Road, for the next connection from Queen's Quay left at 22.20. This was worked by a three-car MED set (with power-units *32* and *33*) and was dull but on time into Bangor. From the station, I still had a good two-mile walk to the Ballymaconnell Road before the day's travels would be completed.

Wednesday 23 July

Instead of leaving Lisburn on the 12.15, I left Bangor on the 12.00 to Queen's Quay, courtesy of a three-car set with cars *16* and *31*. This unit was a bit more lively (new gearboxes!) and managed 61 mph before Holywood and 58 mph on the next section to Sydenham. Before leaving Bangor, I'd 'splashed out' at Boots' chemists and purchased one of their own-label colour transparency films, the price of which included processing. Now, after the almost complete dominance of *50* on the 13.15, you'd have thought it only fair that she turn up for the photo call! However, after the performance on the previous evening, York Road Shed decided to switch engines, and so the photo call belonged to *53*. Not that this was much of a swap – we got 'piston rings blown-*53*' in place of steam-shy *50*. Where was *4* or *55*?

At first it appeared that maybe some remedial work had been done to *53*. The load had also been reduced to seven coaches. So Graham gave us one of the best runs to Antrim for a single-headed train that year – one second under 29 minutes. After a sluggish start to Seaview, and just failing to do 50 mph at Whitehouse by the slimmest of margins, we held 24 mph at Mossley and raced away to 69 mph at Dunadry. We then made a similar start to the previous day to Cookstown Junction, where we almost came to a standstill, only being waved on a the last moment. This then motivated Graham a little more and we touched 60 mph at Kellswater. There were more signal checks before Cullybackey, where, although the diesel was only five minutes late, there was time for a fine photograph of Graham and *53*.

Over the single-line *53* was only marginally better than *50*. Then Graham did an amazing thing – he took the hand tablet exchange at Dunloy at 57 mph (afterwards he admitted "It stubs your arm a bit!") and was away to 64 mph at Post 49, when we were checked by the level crossing gates just beyond Ballyboyland. But for that we might have recorded 21 minutes (instead of 22) over the section to Ballymoney. As on Tuesday, we got 62 mph before the A26 bridge slack. A Portstewart stop and signal check at Dhu Varren ruined progress on the branch, with nothing more than 37 mph and eight minutes late into Platform 3.

On the run home, the weakness caused by *53*'s blown rings was becoming apparent again. As far as Ballymoney *53* was generally behind *50*'s effort of the previous evening, with 49 mph on the Portrush branch and just 51 mph after Macfin. Thereafter *53* was better – probably because the nature of her problem was more of a steady slight loss of power unlike *50*, which had steaming problems and just ended up 'completely winded'. The run up Ballyboyland was not wonderful, but we did succeed in doing 36 mph at the cabin, with a minimum of 32 mph after. Graham was continuing to 'stub his arm', taking the exchange at Dunloy at 43 mph. Thereafter we did 56 mph at Glarryford and 57 mph round Dunminning and the time of 25 m 51 s to Cullybackey was over a minute better than the previous evening. Speed was no more that 47 mph before Ballymena, where, despite having only seven coaches, we still took water. The big weak blast, caused by the blown piston rings, was quite apparent as we made a valiant effort towards Kellswater. From a maximum of 62 mph Graham held over 58 mph over Post 26 only to be rewarded for his efforts by a signal check at Cookstown Junction. After Antrim *53* was in trouble – though not as much as *50* had been in. We were up to 46 mph at Dunadry, fell to 42 mph at the Airport Road crossing and recovered to 45 mph after Templepatrick. But we fell badly over the next three miles to below 35 mph at

Kingsbog. Thereafter we were allowed to accelerate to 60 mph at Mossley. Then a series of bad signal checks impeded progress and we eventually reached York Road 11 minutes late. Today *53* had been in some trouble – but it was nothing compared to what would happen next day.

Thursday 24 July

It was Graham's day off, so WJ Gillespie filled his role. Engine *53* was given another outing – this time with the load restored to eight coaches. Three principle factors had a bearing on the day that was about to unfold. Firstly, the problem of the blown piston rings worsened as the day wore on. Secondly, as previously noted, Gillespie was a driver who tended to reflect the health of his engine – and *53* was in poor shape. Thirdly, we had the extra coach to contend with.

We were already six minutes late when we got the right away from York Road. An abysmal maximum of 40 mph at Whitehouse was followed by an equally poor minimum of under 14 mph on the bank. Then followed a maximum of just 55 mph at Dunadry, all serving to lose us nearly another four minutes. Against this the maximum of 43 mph before the Cookstown Junction stop was actually quite bright, but nothing more than 52 mph was managed at Kellswater. For a change we were now in danger of keeping the diesel waiting, so Gillespie ran up to Cullybackey quite brightly (with a maximum of 35 mph). The stop, which sometimes occupied 20 minutes, was reduced to just 27 seconds! Five more minutes were lost on to Ballymoney, with nothing more than 53 mph down Ballyboyland. Things brightened a little on to Coleraine, with 56 mph before the slack and under 12 minutes on the branch (maximum 44 mph), bringing us into Portrush some 14 minutes late.

Things were so depressing that I decided I'd be better off with a half decent run on the 17.30 to Larne, if it happened to be steam (and there were several evenings during the previous week when this had been the case). So, at Portrush, I quickly raced round to Platform 1 and boarded the four-car MPD set (cars *40* and *52*) on the branch train that was leaving immediately for Coleraine. The 15.00 ex-Londonderry was, as on a previous occasion, in the hands of a Hampshire six-car set, with power-units *72* and *75*. This time we were strengthened to eight coaches by addition of an MPD-trailer and 'bogie' van (no doubt the latter was destined for Larne via the 17.30). This load struggled a little and we were eight minutes late into York Road – only to see a diesel sitting at Platform 2. So, there was nothing else to do but return with the same unit (minus bogie van and MPD trailer) to Coleraine on the 18.00 ex-York Road and thence to Portrush by single unit MPD *65*.

If the run up that afternoon was bad, it held nothing to the disaster that was the 19.55 home. Down the coach someone was playing an old blues American railroad song on a mouth organ, and that just about summed up the mood and the progress. We thought *53* was never going to get through Dhu Varren, so 27 mph at Post 66 and a top speed of 42 mph on the branch was mildly flattering! On to Ballymoney and things got worse – with a top speed of 41 mph after Macfin. We struggled up Ballyboyland, eventually touching 31 mph at the cabin and then fell back to 23 mph over Post 49. Gillespie was getting so desperate that at this point he seems to have almost abandoned hope of getting home. He drifted into Dunloy at jogging pace and shouted an instruction to the signalman to relay a message to York Road, requesting some assistance (in the form of a pilot engine). Then we just limped on, speed generally in the low 30s and never more than 38 mph before Cullybackey. We touched the same speed down the hill into Ballymena, where we were now half an hour late. After this, 52 mph at Kellswater and 46 mph up to Post 26, before an unscheduled stop at Cookstown Junction, was positively breath taking! Then we just drifted easily into Antrim. Looking towards Belfast on the down road, a second engine was waiting – York Road had got the message. Very gently, *55*, with Harry Ramsey on the footplate, was coupled to the stricken *53*.

All of this was completed in less than three minutes and then we were away. – so painlessly, in fact, that fellow enthusiast and timer Derek Henderson, who was sitting in one of the North Atlantic side-compartment coaches, had no idea that a second engine had been added! So, in the run about to be described, Derek thought that crippled *53* had simply had a new lease of life! ("Man dear I couldn't believe my eyes when I saw them big speeds… !")

I've said before that Harry Ramsey was not one to 'hammer an engine', but on my last ever run with him he did a little bit of 'hammering' – so much so that there was no 'maximum before Dunadry/minimum at Post 17' sort of pattern. We just kept on accelerating until after Templepatrick, where we were doing just fractionally below 60 mph! Then *55* was eased and a slight signal check at Kingsbog brought speed down to 48 mph at the cabin. Nothing more than 56 mph was achieved down through Mossley, before an extra stop at Whiteabbey, reached in just over 19 minutes from Antrim. This stop was necessary because we were now running so late that the Ballymena guard had to change to the 22.00 ex-York Road at Whiteabbey. Then the two engines ran easily into York Road (reached 37 minutes late). Afterwards, we had some banter – especially over Derek's miscomprehension! I said "Hey Derek wasn't *55* absolutely brilliant hauling eight coaches and *53*!"

With the late running, my first possible connection was the 22.50 to Bangor, instead of the 22.20. This gave me time to reflect. My (Philip Preece's?) runabout ticket was about to expire. Two 'sick' engines kept being rostered for the 13.15, yet York Road didn't seem prepared to give any other a chance. Perhaps I'd have a lazy weekend, before getting back into the fray on Monday. And with that decision I made the biggest mistake of the year!

Friday 25 July

Overleaf is an imaginary postcard from Ballymoney, date-stamped 14.45.

Dear Michael

We're so sorry you didn't make it today, particularly as you've covered every other occasion that has seen steam on the 13.15 this year. Big Graham (aptly assisted by George Gaw) had 50 and eight coaches. This probably will be his last recorded steam run (in 'company' days). He wanted to leave us something to remember him by and fortunately 50 was in her 'Friday' form, rather than her 'Tuesday' form. You know that desperately difficult 20-minute time from Cullybackey to Ballymoney? Well, today it was kept! Here's how he did it: he got 50 away to more than 60 mph before Dunloy, took the hand tablet exchange at exactly the mile-a-minute and then raced down Ballyboyland at 73 mph. See oul' 50 – down one day and up the next! But sure you might have known that!

All for now
Yours in complete sniggers
Smarter than the average enthusiasts

This was probably the best main-line run of the year – and I missed it. Sometimes life just isn't fair!

On 25 July 1969 No 50, with the 13.15, makes the request stop at a somewhat dilapidated Cookstown Junction and then goes on to make the run of the year.

Arrival of the 15.00 ex-Larne Harbour with No 4 on 26 July 1969. An interesting view of Platforms 4 and 5 at York Road.

Saturday 26 July

A spate of diesel failures caused no less than six Larne-line trains to be steam-hauled today – and of course I missed them all. Talk about smart timing! For the record, the 06.45, 10.05, 13.35 and 17.30 were hauled by number *4* while, as earlier noted, *51* worked the 07.55 and 14.05 trains.

We visited grandfather today. It's not easy watching the slow debilitating deterioration of a once fine man. In his day he had been vice principal of the boys' Model School in north Belfast. He had also been a fine footballer and cricketer. Indeed, he had won a cup winner's medal for Cliftonville in the year before they last won the league (before 1998 that is!). Now it was hard to watch him. The series of strokes that had assaulted him for the past six years had initially robbed him of his ability to communicate. Now they were robbing him of even more basic needs.

We came out of that fine building which used to be Crawfordsburn Hospital and looked across Belfast Lough. It was a fine summer's evening –

one of those evenings when the thermals jostle to make far away things seem closer. A plumb of steam could clearly be seen on the opposite side of the Lough, slowly making progress southwest from Whitehead. The Twelfth holiday fortnight was just ending, and a large tribe of holidaymakers was returning from Scotland. Not unexpectedly, the 17.05 boat train from Larne was quite late. The engine, later identified as *51*, was not making much of a run. Not that that mattered, for far in the distance I was observing *51*, very near the end of her passenger workings. The following Monday, while I would be covering *50* in Portrush, the continuing diesel shortage would provide more than the usual ration of steam workings and *51* would head both the 13.50 boat train and the 17.30 to Larne Harbour. From then on she would be destined only to work spoil trains.

Standing on that hillside, contemplating some of the bigger questions about life and death, it is interesting to note that for the first time the pop charts had a distinctly 'Christian feel' to them. Today, Christian pop music is big business, particularly in America. But in July 1969 the band played on – 'That's the way God planned it' and 'Oh happy day!'

Monday 28 July

I took a chance that NIR would keep steam going on the 13.15 and purchased a runabout ticket at Bangor, just before boarding the three-car MED set (with power units *24* and *25*) forming the 12.00 ex-Bangor. At York Road I was in luck, for an eight-coach rake of steam bogies adorned Platform 2.

There was a change of driver but no change of engine, for we were back to *50* again! The driver was Dan McAtamney, a man already noted for not running up a hill, but who would run like the blazes down the other side. Initially that day running was dreadful. There was a problem – *50* had not had her bunker completely refilled and there was some concern whether or not the coal would last out over the 142-mile round journey (including light engine trips). So, after a nearly five-minute late start out of York Road, we got nothing more than 44 mph at Whitehouse and then a diabolically lazy climb (falling to 14 mph at Mossley). We were then almost brought to a standstill by a signal check at Kingsbog – by which time we had managed to take nearly 24 minutes from leaving York Road. Then Dan produced a run down the hill with 71 mph at Dunadry. We clawed back over two minutes on to Ballymena, without doing anything more than 56 mph at Kellswater. We took water and made another lazy climb to Cullybackey, where the diesel did not keep us waiting too long! The start out of Cullybackey was distinctly better and we managed just over 55 mph before Dunloy. There were no heroics here – the hand tablet exchange was taken at a speed just under half of Graham's record! But another fast run down Ballyboyland (maximum 67 mph) netted a time of just over 22 minutes. (One starts to see just how important that 'massive' hand exchange was to Graham's record of the previous Friday.) So it was on to Coleraine and we achieved 58 mph before the bridge slack. Dan also raced across the Portrush branch in 10 m

41 s, with 49 mph at Post 66, to bring the last ever steam-hauled 13.15 in just six minutes late.

The run home was similar in structure. In an attempt to save fuel, we made a start out of Portrush almost as slow as *53*'s on the previous Thursday! Then we managed 44 mph before a stop at the University. Perhaps more noteworthy was 35 mph and a sub-three minute timing for the little section (actually just over one mile in length) between University and Coleraine! Then followed another fuel-conserving run to Ballymoney, with no more than 46 mph at Macfin and an easy run up Ballyboyland (34 mph at the cabin and 31 mph at Post 49). But Dan would run down a hill even when quite close to a stop, so we actually exceeded 57 mph after Post 38, i.e. just a mile before Cullybackey. From here things improved – someone had obviously looked in the bunker and decided that fuel conservation time was now over. So we managed 50 mph before the stop in Ballymena reached in 5 m 37 s from Cullybackey. At this stage we were running 11 minutes late, but Dan made one of the best starts out to Kellswater that year. We passed there in nine seconds under six minutes doing 64 mph, held 59 mph over Post 26 and touched 64 mph again before Antrim, reached in a respectable 13 m 35 s from Ballymena. The run as far as Monkstown was also good, with 48 mph at Dunadry, 43 mph over the steepest part of the bank, 48 mph at Templepatrick and 44–45 mph sustained right up to Kingsbog. Then Dan raced away to 65 mph at Mossley, before a series of severe signal checks ruined the final run in. The time in from Antrim was still time-keeping at 29 m 32 s, but without the checks this could have been four minutes less and might have made our final deficit just five instead of nine minutes.

Tuesday 29 July

Today involved the reverse moves of the previous Tuesday. I would leave Bangor, travel to Portrush (steam permitting) and return to Lisburn that evening. My family would return to Lisburn by car. So it was out of Bangor on the 12.00 (three-car MED set with power-units *32* and *33*). I would not return to Bangor for some time, but it had been a pleasant change commuting to there everyday, instead of Lisburn.

Then the inevitable happened – the diesel shortage was over. Furthermore, the eight-coach train of the previous day had been fairly sparsely populated – nothing that a five- or six-car diesel couldn't handle. And that was the end of steam on the 13.15. A bit dejected, I made my way to Ballycarry on the 13.50 boat train. Here at least I had a tranquil day, periodically photographing spoil trains on the 'single line' section (see page 100).

Afterwards, I returned to York Road with the hope that at least the 17.30 would be steam. But it was all to no avail – the diesel shortage seemed to have been fully rectified. And so a pattern for the rest of the week emerged. I would turn up at York Road in the forlorn hope of steam on the 13.15 to Portrush, to find that it would be a diesel. I would then use my runabout ticket to photograph spoil trains in the 'Larne Lough' area, returning in the vain hope of steam on the 17.30 to Larne. That didn't happen either. By evening I'd be reduced to timing diesels on the former GN section, long after the 'angel in blue' had gone home. Now that was a fate worse than death!

And the band played softly on: 'Peaceful', 'No Matter What Sign Your Are' and 'Falling In Love Again'.

August 69

Saturday 2 August

This was yet another early start, catching the 07.07 from Lisburn to Great Victoria Street and thence by foot to York Road. At least the 07.55 was steam-hauled, with *53* back in some sort of reasonable form and John Weatherup the driver of two weeks previous. With eight coaches, the run was also similar to that of *51*, with just over 44 mph before Whiteabbey and nothing more than 32 mph before the Greenisland stop. Then we got an even more severe dose of Weatherup's downhill work, with 64 mph exceeded through the Mount. This morning we made stops at both Barn and Kilroot, but still managed a respectable 49 mph before Whitehead. Speeds in excess of 45 mph before Ballycarry, 47 mph before Magheramorne and 44 mph before Glynn were also reasonable work for the load and slightly more sprightly than *51*'s effort. Even on the short section on to Larne we just shaded 40 mph. York Road seemed to have done a reasonable job with the engine since the events of just over a week ago.

Then I did a strange thing. I got off the train at Larne Town and took a diesel back to Belfast (three-car MED set with power-cars *18* and *23*). In doing so I surely forfeited the steam run back on the 09.40 boat train. Thirty years on and I've tried to remember why I might have done this, though I think the explanation is as follows.

It wasn't yet crystal clear what York Road shed intended to do about the following Monday, which was the big Derry holiday. In previous years, a steam train would have been despatched as a relief to Portrush on that Saturday morning. It would not have returned to Belfast, but would then have run empty to Londonderry (maybe carrying the odd enthusiast!). At Derry some extra coaches would have been added for Monday's seaside trip. In 1968, the Monday workings had involved engine *51* and a load of no less than 11 coaches (and some very smart work considering this). Only later that morning did the new NIR rationale become evident. Yes, there would be steam coaches sent to Derry, but they would not be hauled by a steam engine. Instead, individual Hampshire units would haul the rake. After all, didn't you know that a single Hampshire unit (equivalent in power to one 80-class or one 450-class power-unit) was just as good as a steam engine! The deficit in diesels at York Road would be overcome by making some York Road turns steam – notably the 06.45 boat train and 17.30 business express to Larne and also the 09.45 which, for that day only, would be a through train to Portrush, returning at 19.55.

It was a pity that this had not been clear beforehand, for I had just mortgaged a return steam boat train. However, events took a turn that enabled me to clawing back the deficit before the end of the day!

The 14.05 boat train was also steam with *53*, but a reduced load of six coaches. This enabled George Greer to produce one of the best runs I ever had on this train. A good start to Seaview was followed by 51 mph at Whitehouse, a minimum of 43 mph at Bleach Green and then a steady 47–48 mph 'pound' up the hill to the stop in Greenisland in exactly ten and a half minutes. I always reckoned that ten minutes to pass there was very good, so this time to stop has to be seen in a similar vein. A speed of 56 mph at the Mount and 4 m 48 s to Carrickfergus was fine too.

Another good start ensured a sub-seven-minute timing on to Whitehead, with a maximum of 58 mph round the curves. The run on to Larne was not quite as breathtaking, with 47 mph attained before and after Ballycarry.

Then we unexpectedly got a deserved bonus. Because the Hampshire cars had swallowed up many of the steam coaches, while leaving something of a deficit of diesels, the present rake was much too precious to be held in Larne Harbour for the next three or so hours. (A conservative estimate was that the boat from Stranraer was running an hour late.) Also, the deficit of diesels had resulted in over-crowding on the 15.00 stopping boat train. So, *53* quickly made all the manoeuvres necessary to shunt round a rake of coaches at Larne Harbour and we got under way for Belfast, with what was billed as a 15.30 'Relief Passenger', making the same list of stops as the 15.00. Running was fairly dull – Greer almost treated it like a stopping 'empty coaches' run. So we only managed 38 mph before Glynn, 39 mph before Magheramorne and 46 mph on the longer section to Ballycarry. The best

of the work was 37 mph up the hill to Whitehead. We just touched 53 mph at Eden, before signals ruined the run in to Carrickfergus and the run up the Mount was mediocre, with just over 37 mph at Trooperslane. After Whiteabbey, Greer did 52 mph at Whitehouse and then just trundled in to the terminus. At least *53* was out of trouble!

Since *53* had had to make an emergency run back to Belfast a substitute had to be found for the boat train. So *50* was sent down to Larne Harbour with a set of empty coaches.

The coaches were then shunted and, with the arrival of the 15.00 from Londonderry, an extra bogie van was added, taking the load to seven. A different engine and driver were provided for the 17.30. The combination was number *10* with Paddy Dobbin. I say number *10* with some reluctance, for it was almost impossible to read beyond the grime of NIR's filthiest, most rundown-looking machine. RM Arnold talks about her appaling appearance at Easter that year, but since then her footplate had accidentally been set on fire. This had left a gaping hole in the middle, so the poor fireman had, in effect, to

Passing trains at Whitehead on 2 August 1969. No 50, with the 17.05 boat train to York Road, passes 10, with the 17.30 Larne Harbour, on what was probably the last occasion that two steam passenger trains passed on double track.

Unloading mails at Larne Harbour. To facilitate this, 10 *has run forward into the extension platform, thereby pulling the mail coach across the road for ease of access.*

'walk the plank' while trying to fire the engine. Today, health and safety regulations would surely have condemned her. Here was the most pathetic evidence of the demise of steam. In fairness, the run out to Whitehead was not bad. Dobbin managed 49 mph out the lough shore, held 41 mph over Bleach Green and 43–44 mph up to Greenisland. Running down the hill and we just touched 58 mph to bring us into Carrickfergus in a respectable 14 m 51 s. We also managed 53 mph at Post 13, before a signal stop outside Whitehead ruined matters somewhat. After the harsh stop, *10* had trouble blowing the brake off and we took an eternity making the start (past where the RPSI now have their headquarters) to Post 15. We just managed 40 mph before Ballycarry and 46 mph before Magheramorne (the Saturday 17.30 stopped at all stations after Whitehead). After this we just exceeded 40 mph before Glynn and 37 mph before Larne.

To make matters worse, two four-wheeled vans (45 mph variety) were added for the run home. Rubbing brakes were a constant problem, though this may have been because *10* hadn't

enough steam to blow them off. At first things weren't too bad, with 41 mph between Glynn and Magheramorne and particularly 49 mph on to Ballycarry (reached in 5 m 50 s) – quite good for a train of this size. Then we had a serious brake failure and took over five and a half minutes to reach Whitehead. The starts were extremely laborious, though once under way things improved a little, with 49 mph at Kilroot. But after Carrickfergus *10*'s world caved in. We were struggling up through the Mount, at just over 18 mph, when timer Irwin Pryce came down the train and remarked in jocular fashion "Oh we're getting one of those MPD-runs up here tonight!" Running at no more than 28 mph before Greenisland, the non-stop run in from there was ruined by signals at Seaview, though before that Dobbin had at least exceeded 56 mph at Whitehouse.

It seemed a sad finale for what had been an excellent engine, both on the Larne and Bangor lines (readers should refer to RM Arnold's *Steam over Belfast Lough*). Never one for the heavy long distance train, *10* could always run as well as the best on short sharp sprints, like Belfast to Bangor West or Belfast to Carrickfergus. But given her state of repair and today's performance, surely no right-thinking shed foreman would ever permit her to work a passenger train again.

Sunday 3 August

A new phrase (or maybe just a dusted off expression) appeared in the everyday vocabulary of Northern Ireland. Overnight there had been sporadic incidents of sectarian violence. The storm clouds were gathering.

Monday 4 August

I arose early for what would be a big day. Plans had already been made which, with a few modifications, were adhered to. Those plans necessitated me having access to my old bicycle, so before six o'clock I quietly opened the garage door beside our house in Whitla Road, and set forth for York Road. It was a damp drizzly sort of morning, but at least the wind was from the south-west which meant that I cycled the nine miles to York Road in comfortably under half an hour. There I purchased runabout ticket number five and headed towards Platform 2. Despite the early hour there was already a good turnout of enthusiasts, including the redoubtable Mac Arnold. Already late, the engine appeared from the shed. In the gloom we could just about make the engine out, though none of us really believed it, for York Road shed had sent number *10* down! Driver RJ Simpson, always a man to call a spade a spade, didn't believe it either. He immediately got on the internal telephone to the shed and gave forth his wrath in no uncertain terms. (The exact nature of the exchange is not reprinted for it was solidly 'x-rated'!) Removing the expletives, let me say that he was diligently enquiring as to the manner in which he was expected to perform express passenger duties with this dangerous heap of scrap! York Road shed replied that there were no other engines available and he'd better make the best of it.

We all groaned, for surely now RJ would get his own back on the shed foreman by making an embarrassingly bad run, holding other traffic up and then saying that he'd told them so. The load, at five coaches, was not heavy. However, even after we got away some 12 minutes late, we almost immediately had to contend with a signal check, which meant we took over four minutes out to Seaview. That finally seemed to fire RJ (who was affectionately known as the 'Batman'), for quite simply he went out the lough shore in a manner that underscored his nickname. Assisted by fireman Aubrey Ryans, he exceeded 57 mph at Whitehouse, thus establishing my steam record for a train with a load of more than three coaches, and stopped in Whiteabbey in just 4 m 15 s for the three and a third miles from Post 1. The run up to Greenisland was marvellous too, with 46 mph and a time to stop of 4 m 29 s. This train had a Trooperslane stop – we achieved almost 44 mph before and 46 mph after this. After Carrickfergus we had a Barn stop. Unsure of whether passengers from rear coaches wished to detrain, RJ made a 'crockered start', but then raced away to 58 mph round the Whitehead curves and a time of just over seven minutes. At Whitehead the arrears had been cut to just over nine minutes and we made a modestly easy run to Ballycarry, with nothing more than 44 mph. But then we raced away to 51 mph before crossing a diesel at Magheramorne loop. Because we were late, a stop here was not required and we pulled on into the station just beyond. We just about touched 47 mph before Glynn and perhaps more noteworthy was a massive 45 mph between Glynn and Larne Town. At the Harbour terminus we were just under five minutes late.

Unfortunately, the amount of marshalling required to turn an engine round a train at Larne Harbour cannot be achieved in the ten minutes we were allowed that morning. So the 07.55 ex-Larne Harbour was almost ten minutes late away. But there was more sharp work, with 30 mph before the Town, 44 mph before Glynn and 48 mph before Magheramorne. We also just shaded 55 mph on the section from Magheramorne to Ballycarry (reached in 5 m 32 s). A smart start was made to Whitehead, with 39 mph early on,

No 10 is pictured on arrival at York Road with the 07.55 ex-Larne Harbour on 4 August 1969. Note the diesel hydraulic shunter, No 1, marshalling a railcar in Platform 2. No 1 had been in service for just four days.

but then RJ eased number *10* and speculation mounted that her steaming problems had reappeared. For all that, the rest of the run was not bad, with less than seven and a half minutes to Carrickfergus (maximum of 55 mph at Eden). By then we were just six minutes late. We were also away smartly up the hill, with 43 mph before Greenisland (passed in 5 m 23 s from Carrickfergus), but then a series of signal checks, including a complete standstill at Whiteabbey, ensured nothing more than 53 mph before York Road, and a final deficit of nearly nine minutes. But *10* had proved her worth – the engine of the short sharp shift!

The next steam run scheduled that memorable day was the 09.45 to Portrush. For this, *53* and seven coaches were provided and along with them, John Scott! Well, we got a typical John Scott start – just exceeding 36 mph at Whitehouse and by this stage we were anticipating falling to single figures on the bank. Certainly it seemed that way, when we were down to 25 mph by Whiteabbey. Then Scott seemed to 'catch himself on', as they say. He opened *53* up ever so slightly, so that speed fell to a minimum

of 18 mph just after Monkstown, but then slowly recovered and by Kingsbog Junction we were doing 31 mph. Notably this was not the slowest run of the day up through Monkstown – the MPD set on the 14.50 to Derry was noted falling to 17 mph! Now, having notched the engine up, Scott did not bother changing the setting, with the result that we raced away to 67 mph at Templepatrick. Then he suddenly noticed what he was doing and applied the brakes for a more typical rate of 53 mph round Dunadry! We'd taken over 35 minutes to Antrim, but it had been entertaining. On to Ballymena he did run up to Post 26 at 43–44 mph and was away to over 53 mph before Post 28, when signals at Kellswater ruined all further progress.

At Ballymena we took water and driver John Doherty from Derry relieved Scott. He made a bright run up to the Cullybackey stop (maximum 38 mph) and the run on to Ballymoney was not bad either, except for the painstakingly slow hand tablet exchange at Dunloy. Before this he had exceed 54 mph and he just about touched 59 mph down Ballyboyland. This train had a fairly harsh timing, so by now we were 21 minutes

By 1969 the only other working steam engine that NIR possessed was ex-SLNCR 0-6-4T No 27 Lough Erne. She survived because her short wheelbase permitted movement over sidings that connected the main line to Belfast Docks. On 4 August she is seen propelling empty wagons en route to collect coal supplies. The arrival of the diesel hydraulic shunter sealed her fate and she was last steamed under the NIR banner on 21 October 1969. She is now preserved by the RPSI.

late. The A26 bridge slack was also painstakingly observed, though we'd touched 56 mph beforehand.

At Coleraine I said goodbye to my mates and went off for some well deserved 'brunch' in the little cafe opposite the station, which still serves up the same sort of goodies to this day. I could have gone on to Portrush, but I had other important business to attend to, which for once meant forgoing a few steam miles. For today the A' level results were published and back in 1969 you did not get such things sent by post – you had to turn up at the school in person and receive notification of your fate! So, it was my intention to return to Belfast by diesel, cycle to school to get that one result I was waiting for and then travel all the way back to Portrush. However, before doing that I would take the opportunity of checking what happening to the 17.30, which was also due to be steam. An alternative plan was to take the 17.30 to Whitehead, get back to York Road by diesel from whence I could still make it as far as Ballymoney to meet *53*. In the event it was the alternative plan which was called upon.

But first there was the cycle run to Methody, where the grade A (in Mathematics) which I had so much hoped for, eventually became a reality. Afterwards, I celebrated with a can of Coca Cola from the fridge in Woolworths, before cycling the last section back to York Road.

At York Road I met up with my young friend Robert White. The driver for the 17.30 that week was Thomas Crymble of Carrickfergus, who even today can still be frequently seen making the journey between Greenisland and his home. Aubrey Ryans was certainly getting his fair share of firing passenger trains, for he too was on the 17.30 all week (after covering the 06.45 that morning). Unbelievably, York Road had yet again produced number *10*, so the decision to cover this turn as far as Whitehead was cemented. While RJ had been outspoken about the selection of engine, quiet Tommy just shook his head. I had a few words with him before we left – to encourage him by saying that despite *10*'s appearance, she had been in fine fettle that morning. It worked! Tommy had the six coaches away to over 52 mph at Whitehouse and then never fell below 47 mph at either Bleach Green or Greenisland. Then he raced away to 63 mph through the Mount to reach Carrickfergus in a fine time of 13 m 56 s. After a slow start, the run on to Whitehead was exemplary too. Tommy just touched 60 mph round the curves and came to a standstill at the seaside town in 7 m 18 s.

There I had to leave, but I had Robert well briefed to keep notes. The run on to Larne was nothing special, and by the return trip the driver, and particularly the fireman, had had enough of avoiding the hole in the floor, at speeds well above those encountered by spoil trains. So at Magheramorne loop, recalling the incident with number *5* on 4 July, poor *10* was substituted by another engine from a spoil train. And that really was the end. She never worked another passenger train, but I was pleased to have recorded her in such grand form right at the very end. As so clearly recorded in *Steam Over Belfast Lough*, she finished as she had always been – the engine most capable of a furious short hop with a moderate or moderately heavy load.

And so it was back to York Road courtesy of a three-car MED set (power cars *18* and *19*). There was plenty of time, too, to make the connection to the 19.10 to Londonderry, which was in the hands of a three-car MPD set (with power units *42* and *45*). This train was eight minutes late away and was not helped by an extra stop at Cookstown Junction, nor a signal check at Kellswater. By Ballymena we were 12 minutes late and I was getting concerned that the race over the ornate metal footbridge at Ballymoney might not be just quite as routine as I'd hoped for. Even at that time, Ballymoney was controlled by an automatic staff system for the single line, and it was one place where the outbound train could be on the move before the inbound had come to a stop, on the opposite platform. So, I decided to go for minimum risk and detrained at Cullybackey for a pleasant summer evening's walk round the village.

Afterwards, Irwin Pryce told me I could have made the Ballymoney connection with impunity – for the guards were exchanged at that stop – but I hadn't realised this at the time. This was the only blot on an otherwise memorable day and it resulted in my missing a nice 63 mph round Dunminning, described by RM Arnold as "something we hadn't seen all summer". But what Mac Arnold does not record is that good running did not end at Cullybackey that night. The final time-tabled (19.55) train ex-Portrush was in the hands of Percy Mitchell, and he was making a good deal more out of *53* than had the drivers of that morning. True, the run down to Ballymena was sedate at no more than 46 mph. But the start out to Kellswater was the best of the year, with a time to pass of exactly six minutes and a speed of 66 mph. Percy then held 60 mph up to Post 26, before signals at Cookstown Junction reduced this pace by more than a third. But we were away again to 60 mph before the Antrim stop, reached in 14 m 38 s.

The climb out of Antrim was just plain good work, with 50 mph at Dunadry and then falling to no more than 46 mph over the worst part of the bank. Then we were away with an unfaltering beat through Templepatrick, again touching 50 mph, before a very limited fall off to Kingsbog brought us past the cabin at 46 mph in 14 m 12 s from Antrim. Thereafter we just drifted downhill before an extra Whiteabbey stop, brought about by late running, which could only be blamed on the performance of the tardy diesel which had forced me to miss the Ballymoney to Cullybackey section. We then managed 55 mph on the final section into York Road, reached just 19 minutes late.

After exchanging pleasantries with the driver and fellow enthusiasts (Percy had been on his best behaviour that day, due to the presence of one of two high ranking NIR officials!), it was a case of retrieving the bike. The intention was not to cycle all the way home though, but just to Great Victoria Street. It was now quite dark and I was very happy to load the machine into the Guard's van of a three-car BUT set (cars *124* and *134*). So it was home at last and the happy job of delivering good news. I wish every day was like this!

(Continued on page 101)

The best units were reserved for the 'Enterprise'. BUT railcars are still on the 14.30 ex-Great Victoria Street at Portadown in July 1968.

Norman Johnston

A little over a year later and the 'Enterprise' seen leaving Great Victoria Street is firmly in the hands of Hampshire units. In the background are BUT and AEC units (the latter has not been painted in red and is probably 115) and diesel-hydraulic shunter number 3.

Norman Johnston

MED railcar set 22-519-23 on the 10.55 York Road to Larne at Carrickfergus on 6 March 1969. The centre coach is a rebuild of an ex-LMS nine compartment non-corridor third.

Norman Johnston

The railcar and steam sheds at York Road, Belfast, on 6 March 1969. On the left is the railcar running shed with MPD railcars and the unique ex-SLNCR 0-6-4T No 27 Lough Erne in steam. In the small engine shed are Nos 55 and 10, whilst to the right No 3 takes water. This entire area is now under the M2/M5 motorway.

Norman Johnston

The regular 13.15 ex-York Road approaching University on 15 July 1969. No 4 is hauling ten bogies. This locomotive is now preserved by the RPSI.

CP Friel

The scene at Portrush on the evening of 15 July 1969. No 50 is departing on the six bogie 18.40 to Coleraine, whilst No 53 waits at Platform 3 with the 20.10. No 4 takes water and a five-car '70 class' has the 19.25. This set was strengthened by three ex-NCC bogie coaches. No 50 returned from Coleraine to work another train.

CP Friel

A typical scene of the 17.30 ex-York Road at Whitehead. On 6 August No 53 is in bunk-first mode and the ex-GNR bogie 'P' van taken off the 15.00 ex-Londonderry forms the first vehicle. The second is an ex-GNR J11 tricomposite brake. CP Friel

Devoid of passenger duties, No 51 passes a stationary No 4, both on stone trains at Ballycarry on 29 July 1969. No 51 went on to produce the highest mileage of any jeep in the year 1969–70.

Author

(Continued from page 96)

Tuesday 5 August

York Road shed loved number *4* – she was the favourite. They would always send her out immaculately – when you couldn't read the number on the front buffer beam of many another! Here comes *4*, sunshine glinting off her red buffer beam. If *10*, a complete wreck, could manage a good run yesterday, shouldn't this engine be great? And that was always where I got it wrong – appearances can be deceptive! All the way out to Larne on the 17.30, *4* and her six coaches were distinctly dull. Tommy did nothing more than 46 mph at Whitehouse and fell below 36 mph at Bleach Green. True, 41 mph at Greenisland and 58 mph down the Mount was livelier, but it still didn't compete with the effort by *10*. The time of 7 m 52 s on to Whitehead was marred by a poor stop, though we did exceed 57 mph round the curves at Post 13. Rubbing brakes, which had caused the bad stop into Whitehead (or was *4* not steaming too well?), meant that we didn't manage 40 mph before Ballycarry nor 50 mph after that.

The run home, with *4* now characteristically facing chimney first, was better, despite the addition of two four-wheeled vans. We were eight minutes late out of the Harbour station. Now just exceeding 37 mph before Glynn and not quite 40 mph before Magheramorne were no records, but the time of 5 m 45 s from there to Ballycarry was snappier than the top speed of just over 47 mph suggested. Just 35 mph before Whitehead did not bode particularly well for the rest of the journey. But Tommy produced a little more steam for the run to Carrickfergus, reached in 7 m 24 s, with a maximum speed of 58 mph at Downshire Park. The uphill work was not too bad, with 39 mph after Trooperslane and a time of 6 m 17 s to stop in Greenisland. Anyone joining there got the best of it – for Tommy managed over 45 mph before the Jordanstown stop (in 2 m 49 s) and 36 mph before Whiteabbey (in 2 m 36 s). There then followed a little bit of 'fireworks' along the lough shore, where 61 mph was exceeded and York Road reached with the same deficit with which we had left Larne Harbour.

Wednesday 6 August

Although Monday was the big Derry holiday day, at least one diesel set was retained there for daily Portrush workings during the rest of the week. That in turn ensured regular steam on the 17.30 ex-York Road. The array of engines was interesting too. Tonight *53*, alias York Road's second favourite engine, turned up – again notice that you can nearly always read her buffer beam number from the photographs! Overall though, we got much more running. The six-coach train started very well with 53 mph at Whitehouse, followed by holding 44 mph at Bleach Green, a race away to almost 50 mph at Jordanstown and 46 mph over the summit at Greenisland. We were four seconds under ten minutes to pass the former junction, so Tommy eased down the hill with just 58 mph after Trooperslane. Nevertheless, 13 m 38 s to Carrickfergus was an excellent time, and we were now actually running a minute early. A speed of 55 mph on to Whitehead maintained this margin (see page 100). We then managed 45 mph before the Ballycarry stop, 48 mph before the Magheramorne loop slack and almost touched 55 mph at Glynn. Larne and Larne Harbour were both reached spot on time. On nights like this, the regular patrons must have wished that steam would continue to replace the unreliable diesels for years to come. Sadly, this was not to be the case.

With no extra vans to complicate matters, we were treated to a fine example of how to get the return of the 17.30 (the 19.15 ex-Larne Harbour) into York Road almost two minutes early! Tommy did it this way. Less than a minute late away, we managed a reasonable 29 mph before the Town Station and 39 mph before Glynn. Then the running really started, for Tommy had *53* away to 46 mph before the Magheramorne stop (in 3 m 48 s) and almost touched 55 mph before the Ballycarry stop (in 5 m 25 s). The run up to Whitehead was one of my best, with over 40 mph and a time of 3 m 50 s. Tommy produced a fine run on to Carrickfergus too, with 62 mph at Downshire Park and a time of 7 m 03 s. Now, since 23 May I hadn't had one of those runs up Mount Bank that could be described as 'better that the average 80- or 450-class'. But again *53* obliged, with 37 mph at the Mount and 47 mph before Greenisland reached in 5 m 23 s. Forty-seven mph before the stop at Jordanstown (in 2 m 45 s) and 36 mph before the Whiteabbey stop (in 2 m 36 s) were similar to the previous evening. The final 62 mph sprint along the Lough shore meant that even a severe signal check, outside the terminus, could not falter my best time-keeping effort on the 17.30 and return.

Thursday 7 August

If commuters were well pleased with their treatment on Wednesday, they had cause for complaint on Thursday. This evening Tom Crymble had number *50* and it was to be both my last run with the engine, which had dominated this memorable summer, and her last recorded effort on the Larne line. But first, she had been ill prepared for the journey. Already seven minutes late away, the six-coach train was in trouble right from the start. Tommy nursed her out along the shore, only momentarily exceeding 36 mph. By Bleach Green we were down to 19 mph and all concerned were very glad not to be continuing on the main line. The dip into Jordanstown netted 27 mph and then we fell rapidly to 15 mph before Greenisland. At this stage the run was developing like those runs today, with the 80- and 450-class trains, when the unit has actually cut out (usually due to overheating), but a little bit of electric traction in their capacitors just allows wheels to keep moving! Once over the top, gravity let speed accelerate to 41 mph, before the stop in Carrickfergus in everybody's worst ever time (for steam on this train) of over 23 minutes. By now Tommy had partially pulled the engine round and so 7 m 48 s on to Whitehead, with over 56 mph round the curves was a good bit more encouraging. Just 41 mph before the Ballycarry stop was pretty dull, as was 45 mph before Magheramorne. There we were forced to go

through the slow loop, losing more time in the process. This seemed to inspire Tommy to put *50* through her paces and he managed 58 mph through the Glynn. We were 18 minutes late at Larne, though only two minutes had been lost since Carrickfergus.

We commiserated with fireman Aubrey Ryans at Larne Harbour. Aubrey was the last lad ever to be taken on by the former Ulster Transport Authority as a footplateman. He was very professional in his attitude to his work and magnanimously took the entire blame for *50*'s ill preparedness. "She had the better of me going out...she'll not have the better of me on the way home" he declared! This turned out to be a pretty accurate statement. Overall, *50* was not quite as good as *53* had been on the previous evening, but there was still plenty of noteworthy running. Firstly, there was the added incentive of a 13-minute late departure. Then we exceeded 42 mph on the section between Larne Town and Glynn and 45 mph on to Magheramorne. The jaunt through the slow loop jaded progress on the next section to Ballycarry, with just over 46 mph recorded, and 36 mph before Whitehead was well down on the previous evening. The run into Carrickfergus was completed in just over seven and a half minutes with 56 mph at Kilroot. Things then started to get better, with a fine 44 mph after Trooperslane to reach Greenisland in 5 m 50 s. The rest of the work was well up to the standard of the previous evening, with 46 mph before the Jordanstown stop (in 2 m 42 s), 38 mph before the stop in Whiteabbey (in 2 m 38 s) and a final dash away to 63 mph along the lough shore. Unrestrained by signal checks, the time to stop in York Road of 6 m 39 s was commendable too, as was the fact that we were now just 11 minutes late. Once again, my last run with an engine seemed to be crowned with a little blaze of final glory.

Friday 8 August

All week, the running on the 17.30 business express had been of a high standard, odd problems excepted. On Friday night we were

York Road station circa early 1968. The NIR logo, the presence of a trolley bus and absence of leaves on the trees provide some precision in dating.

privileged to experience arguably my best all round effort on this train, particularly when the load of seven coaches is taken into account. The engine was *53* – the only engine to be repeated that week. Despite the reasonably heavy load, Tommy had us away to Seaview at almost 'diesel pace', and thereafter was much better than an average diesel on the Larne line. We touched 51 mph at Whitehouse, fell to 44 mph at Bleach Green and then held an astounding 48–49 mph over Greenisland, passed in one second over ten minutes. A reasonable sprint took us to 61 mph through the Mount before the stop in Carrickfergus in just 13 m 33 s – overall my second best time, but arguably the best when load is taken into consideration. We then roared away from Carrickfergus, managing 60 mph before the Whitehead curves where Tommy eased to 55–56 mph. The time into Whitehead was three seconds under seven minutes. Even 4 m 08 s on to

Ballycarry was not bad, with 46 mph exceeded. Over the section to Larne Town we managed 52 mph before the Magheramorne loop tablet exchange (taken at 32 mph) and then raced away to 60 mph at the Glynn. Time over this section was also my second best, at four seconds under the relatively hard schedule (including the slack) of ten minutes. The 17.30 was allowed 39 minutes to Larne Town, including the three stops – that evening our running time had been just 34 m 34 s. Including normal station time, this still represented over two minutes gained. Our two-minute late arrival was because of excessive station time at Carrickfergus and all credit was due to engine and crew.

Unfortunately, the load remained at seven coaches for the run home. Even so, 37 mph before the Glynn stop and 44 mph before Magheramorne was not bad. We then had to stop at Magheramorne loop – this time to exchange firemen with a spoil train. After that we managed 49 mph before the Ballycarry stop and 35 mph up the hill to Whitehead. The exchange of fireman had left us almost three minutes late, but Tommy made up some time recording 7 m 28 s to Carrickfergus, without exceeding 55 mph. The extra coach told a little up through the Mount, though we almost touched 40 mph before the Greenisland stop. As on previous evenings, we managed 46 mph on the short easy section to Jordanstown (reached in 2 m 52 s) and 37 mph on to Whiteabbey (reached in 2 m 38 s). The final stretch in along the lough shore was unchecked and so another sub seven-minute time was recorded, with 61 mph at Post 2. So arrival at York Road was just short of two minutes late. Notably Tommy had exceeded 60 mph here on each of the four evenings that I had been present. So near to the end, this was a fine and fitting finale for steam on this train.

Saturday 9 August

The 06.40 ex-Portadown (six-car BUT set with power units *127*, *128* and *131*) left me just three minutes late at Great Victoria Street – sufficient time for a gentle jog across to York Road in the pleasant morning summer sunshine. There was also still time to view the engine heading the 07.55 to Larne Harbour. "Best of a bad lot" I said, somewhat tongue in cheek, on noting that *53* was taking the honours yet again. "He means the engine – not the driver", explained Irwin Pryce to driver Bill Smyth of Larne, who took it all in good heart. He ran with good heart too. With seven coaches he managed 50 mph at Whitehouse and stopped in Whiteabbey in 8 m 22 s. The run up to Greenisland was at a steady 36–37 mph, reached in 5 m 37 s – a good start, followed by an easy 53 mph through the Mount, netting a sub five-minute time to Carrickfergus. Smyth was a driver who would start and finish well – so he would produce his best work on stopping trains such as these. The section on to Whitehead had all these qualities and a time of 7 m 12 s, without exceeding 55 mph. Even smarter was 49 mph between Whitehead and Ballycarry

and a time of 3 m 54 s, bettering Crymble's time of the previous evening. We just failed to touch 50 mph before Magheramorne (reached in 5 m 57 s) and 45 mph before Glynn (reached in 3 m 44 s). Again, Smyth's willingness to keep *53* going to the last possible moment produced 42 mph and a very good time of 3 m 32 s on the section from Glynn to Larne Town. At the Harbour we were just a little over three minutes late – most of which due to the late start from York Road.

The boat passengers were well and truly delayed and we did not get the right away until 10.56, as opposed to a scheduled departure of 09.40. Fortunately, this was a time when there was little restricting us, and Smith got an almost unchecked run to York Road. I say almost, because there was still the two hand tablet exchanges at Magheramorne loop and Ballycarry to deal with, as well as slight signal checks at Magheramorne and Whitehead. On the single line Smyth handled *53* sensibly, managing 50 mph before Magheramorne and 49 mph afterwards. He took the tablet at Ballycarry at 37 mph and maintained a steady 39 mph to Whitehead, passed in just over 16 minutes from the Harbour. To hold the boat train timing now required running the 14.7 miles, from passing Whitehead to York Road, in 19 minutes. Again, steady work at first took us away to 56 mph at Downshire Park. Then *53* was opened up for the Mount bank and held 43–44 mph over Greenisland. The engine was then eased, but still allowed to run with a whisker of steam, so that we just exceeded 64 mph at Whitehouse and made a good stop into York Road in 34 m 29 s from the Harbour – half a minute under schedule.

For the 14.05 boat train, York Road supplied number *55* and a six-coach rake. As on the Saturday just four weeks previous, the driver was Larne man R Kemp. Not much was expected, but in fact we did much better than that! The time of 11 m 46 s to stop in Greenisland was no record, but I can assure you that I had had much worse with Larne men on this train. After just exceeding 46 mph at Whitehouse, Kemp held 38 mph over Bleach Green and 41 mph right up to the back-line crossover, where a sharp application of brakes was made. Over 55 mph through the Mount and a time of 4 m 47 s to Carrickfergus was fairly sharp too. A bad signal check outside Whitehead cost us over a minute. Prior to that, we had been running almost in tandem with *53*'s run that morning and had managed 56 mph before Post 13. Then came another good speed before Ballycarry, this time 48 mph, and a time to stop of 4 m 08 s. The 50 mph watershed was exceeded before the Magheramorne slow loop and station, reached in 5 m 52 s. Almost 45 mph before Glynn (reached in 3 m 46 s) and 38 mph before Larne Town (reached in 3 m 38 s) were not dissimilar to Smyth's effort.

And so, at exactly 15.00, just eight minutes late, *55* reached the Larne Harbour extension platform for the the very last time.

We then headed back to York Road on the 16.05 ex-Larne Harbour (three-car MPD set with power-units *54* and *57*) for, in keeping with the previous Saturday, the 17.30 was due to be steam-hauled. Poor Tom Crymble was getting no rest that week, for he again turned up with *53* and a load stretched to eight coaches. Then, perhaps he wouldn't have had it any other way, for this would be his last passenger turn (under an NIR banner).

For a big train, this one produced very solid stuff. Tommy almost touched 50 mph at Whitehouse and held 41–42 mph at Bleach Green and Greenisland, before a maximum of 55 mph through the Mount and a very worthy time to Carrickfergus of two seconds under the schedule of 15 minutes. On to Whitehead, Tommy managed 55 mph before easing for the curves and a time of 7 m 26 s. A signal stop before Ballycarry ruined that section, but 47 mph before Magheramorne was reasonable, as was nearly 44 mph before Glynn. We didn't quite reach 36 mph before the Town stop and ran in ten minutes late – seven of which was due to a late start from York Road and much of the rest due to the signal stop at Ballycarry. Along the way we had neither passed nor crossed the 17.05 boat train, and this was confirmed as we approached the Harbour. Engine *55* was still sitting at Platform 2, with her

vacuum brakes off and getting ready to move.

My logbook states that the boat train started to move five seconds after the 17.30 came to a halt. It might even have been less than that – indeed some felt we had actually made a negative connection! And some enthusiasts sadly didn't make it across the island platform in time to jump aboard the moving train. This was a pity, for this was one run I would not have liked to have missed. The driver had been changed to John Weatherup, who initially ran very easily, not quite managing 50 mph before Magheramorne and only 46 mph afterwards. Also, he took the hand exchanges very tentatively, and this meant that we'd taken nearly half our allotted time by the time we passed Whitehead. There was 14.7 miles to go and just over 17 minutes to do it. From 42 mph through Whitehead station, Weatherup accelerated steadily and touched 62 mph at Eden. Now, at no time during this run was *55* worked particularly hard. From this great start on level ground, the engine and her six coaches were allowed to fall back to 41–42 mph over Greenisland – though the minimum speed was exaggerated by a slight signal check. Then came the bit that nobody expected. The setting on the engine was scarcely touched and *55* was certainly an engine that would run down a hill! We must have made a fine sight, in days long before theme parks, by racing up the chicane to meet the main line at Bleach Green Junction at 60 mph! And it didn't end there, for Weatherup kept on lightly working *55* until we eventually hit 72 mph at Whitehouse – my biggest speed ever on a Larne line train. Mac Arnold, in *Steam over Belfast Lough*, tells how, prior to 1967, this sort of running in from Greenisland was commonplace. But permanent way restrictions, followed by restriction on steam engines, had ended the day of the near 80 mph dash in along the lough shore. Here, at the very end, *55* and Weatherup were showing us just how easily it could be done, for you could hardly have heard *55* all day. As we came to a halt, my watch stopped at 34 m 37 s – he'd taken just over 17 minutes in from Whitehead. So I had experienced two schedule-keeping steam boat trains in one day, and by this time next week they'd be confined to history. Notably, *55* became the last jeep in 'company days' to exceed 70 mph.

Derek Henderson offered me a lift in his car back to Greenisland to catch Tommy's (and *53*'s, on the Larne line) last fling, but I declined. My mother's only brother, Ronnie, his wife Joan and my four cousins had just arrived home for an infrequent holiday. So it would have been churlish of me not to head for home immediately. But what a fine day it had been.

Looking back, this was a wonderful week. If I could ever have wished time to stop, it was then. Just a year before, British Rail had ended all steam operations and, in addition to all the local enthusiasts, Northern Ireland Railways had had the revenue from a fair sprinkling of disenfranchised English 'spotters'. They had been much impressed by the standard of operation that was being handed out daily. The British Railways 80000 class is a far distant, more modern and more powerful cousin of the jeeps. But there was little doubt that running of the standard seen in this past week, would not have been common place with these engines, now Britain's most preserved steam class. Yet, by the end of that week, four of the jeeps – *10*, *50*, *53* and *55* – would never work another recorded passenger turn on the Larne line.

In other ways too it was an idyllic week – so much in contrast with the one to come.

Monday 11 August

Thankfully the weekend had passed off with little further report of violence. The papers, however, were full of impending gloom over the Apprentice Boys' march which was due to be held in Derry on the next day. This had in the past been a great occasion for steam enthusiasts, with as many as six special steam trains converging on the maiden city. A report in the *Belfast Telegraph* this evening, indicated that there was some evidence of people choosing to stay away. An NIR spokesman indicated that they were catering for approximately 2,500 people. This was

somewhat below previous years, but was probably a blessing in disguise – for I doubt if NIR could have transported previous years' volumes. Compared with 1968, they were two steam engines short and both lost engines, *3* and *56*, had worked specials. Moreover, there was the state of repair of some of the existing engines to contend with. Rival transport firm Ulsterbus said they would be transporting roughly the same number of people as in previous years.

To handle the reduced traffic, NIR had come up with a plan that kept steam to a minimum. Firstly, the regular 08.10 and 09.45 trains would be considerably strengthened and worked by MPD units. Secondly, as in the case of the Derry holiday specials, extra trains from Belfast would use single Hampshire cars, dragging steam coaches behind. This left steam confined to the specials starting from Antrim and Ballymena respectively.

Tuesday 12 August

There were rumours of additional steam turns on the Larne line, so I left home even earlier than on the previous Monday and cycled to York Road. The ticket barrier was closed and so I travelled to Carrickfergus on the 06.15 (three-car MPD unit with power cars *60* and *64*) where I purchased my final runabout ticket of the summer. The crossing keeper at Jordanstown had not turned up, so driver Rab Graham insured progress by personally opening the gates! No 'feeder trains' were steam hauled and so I returned to York Road on the 06.28 ex-Larne Harbour, courtesy of a four-car MED set (power units *13* and *22*).

The 08.10 to Londonderry was, as anticipated, a nine-car MPD set (power units *41*, *43*, *51*, *52*, *55* and *59*). At Antrim jeep *55* was being hooked up to a set of eight coaches. So an engine that hadn't got beyond Antrim all July was the choice for the last steam train to Derry. Engine *4* had already been despatched to Ballymena for a special leaving there at 09.05. Interspersed were the 'Hampshire' specials. Their progress was unlikely to be lively and, with the volume of traffic, this would dictate the pace. So, there was absolutely no incentive for driver Davie McDonald to do any running at all. We got away on schedule at 09.15 and trundled to Ballymena as if this were an empty coaches working, not doing anything more than 48 mph at Kellswater. Then we were signal checked before the Cullybackey stop, where we had a further pick-up of passengers and also had to cross the 08.15 ex-Londonderry. This meant that it was 10.00 before we were under way from there. McDonald made a very weak climb up to Post 38 and nothing more than 45 mph before the Glarryford stop. From there we did at least exceed 50 mph before a very slow hand tablet exchange at Dunloy. These were probably delaying techniques to ensure that the train in front was well and truly cleared. The tactic worked – Davie got a clear run to Ballymoney and had a last ever steam sprint down Ballyboyland at 67 mph.

There was method in what the driver had done so far. The tanks had only been topped up at Ballymena, and 55 needed to run the 62 miles to Londonderry without further replenishment. Knowing he would be held up during the earlier part of the run, Davie had sought to conserve water. From Ballymoney, the final steam train to Derry was booked to run non-stop. This was actually done very efficiently, for the 42 miles were completed in a minute under the hour, despite seven speed restrictions en route – the A26 bridge slack, Coleraine station and hand tablet exchanges at Castlerock, Bellarena, Limavady Junction, Eglinton and Lisahally. Additionally, there was a permanent way restriction in force between Eglinton and Culmore. Engine 55 managed just 52 mph before the A26 slack, 49 mph between Coleraine and Castlerock, 57 mph before Bellarena, 53 mph before Limavady Junction and just 50 mph before Eglinton. A final maximum of 48 mph was reached after Lisahally and then the final brake application of a Derry-bound steam train brought us into the terminus at 11.31. After Saturday's efforts this run was dull but efficient and it was fitting for 55 to join 4 on this sad occasion.

After the Apprentice Boys had disappeared on buses towards the city centre, Alex Lindsay and I stepped out on to Duke Street. It was a perfectly still, grey morning. There wasn't another living soul in the street. It was eerie – the ultimate calm before the storm. We decided to use our runabout tickets and stay out of the city during the day. First though, 55 had to be turned on the turntable, soon never to be used again.

Just behind the turntable were rows of little houses. The Protestant Waterside community was fortunate in not residing in multi-story flats, which marked the Catholic Brandywell estate. They were fortunate in not reaping the social ills that are now well documented about this type of accommodation. But the little 'two-up, two-down' dwellings they did inhabit could scarcely be described as living in the lap of luxury.

We made our way back towards the station, stopping only to photograph 4 taking water at the water tower.

Then it was back to Belfast, Alex and I using the 12.30 ex-Derry as a convenient way to catch up on lost sleep! This train was composed of four MPD power cars (38, 40, 55 and 59) and four four-wheeled vans. Apparently not all power-units were functioning, for we could manage no more than 31 mph at Ballyboyland cabin and also fell to 32 mph before Kingsbog Junction. We had a bite to eat and returned to Derry on the 16.00, the MPD set now reduced to three units – 40, 55 and 59 – so one may guess who the culprit was! We halted just outside Waterside, to let the first steam special exit from the platform we were booked to arrive in. Bertie Wright, 55 and the eight-coach rake moved past on the lough side to our right, destined for Antrim. Due out at 19.05, just fifteen minutes behind 55, Paddy Dobbin had 4 and a nine-coach train. On time, the last steam train slid out of Waterside, most of the occupants probably more taken up with the day's events than railway history in the making. There was no trouble on board this train, indeed reports afterwards generally praised the Apprentice Boys for restraint, despite provocation during the march. However, the event had been high-jacked by an increasingly militant Civil Rights

The booking hall within the concourse of York Road station, from whence many an adventure started!

Association, whose fight was with the forces of law and order in Northern Ireland, whom they saw as partial towards loyalism and loyalists. So the day became the catalyst for further acts of violence, and running battles with the police raged on into the night.

Paddy Dobbin did not rage home. The run was even duller than the morning's effort. We didn't quite touch 53 mph before a stop in Limavady Junction. We also made a short stop at Castlerock to cross the 18.00 ex-York Road. As in the morning, the best of the running was between Magilligan and Downhill, with 55 mph exceeded just at the point where you get the most magnificent views (from the non-milepost side that is!). We also exceeded 51 mph on the section from Castlerock to Coleraine, where we were signal-checked and another stop was made. Again, the problem will have been labouring Hampshire units with loads they weren't actually designed to haul. We just failed to do 50 mph before another stop at Ballymoney. Up Ballyboyland and 33 mph at the signal-cabin (31

mph minimum afterwards) was still faster that the MPD unit had managed earlier in the day! Even with this, we were still brought down by signals at Dunloy. It really was just a case of getting the people home – somehow! On the final section to Ballymena we managed 53 mph round Dunminning and 51 mph after the Cullybackey hand tablet exchange.

Nobody invited any of us to travel on the empty coaches and so it was a case of catching the last diesel to York Road – the 19.55 ex-Portrush, altered to 20.15 for the occasion and still considerably late. The tardy four-car MED unit encountered much earlier in that day, worked this run.

I finish with one amusing story on a day somewhat devoid of humour. Dobbin and *4* were just approaching Glarryford, at a mere 48 mph when an English enthusiast miscalculated the speed and penned the word 'FANTASTIC' in block capitals into his logbook. I tell you, those English steam engines must have been dull in the extreme for this run to warrant such an accolade!

Wednesday 13 August

Today was my brother's 12th birthday. He wasn't having friends in, or anything dreadfully social like that, so I took him with me to York Road. Dan McAtamney was back on the 17.30 turn and I'm glad to report that for Paul's birthday the train was steam-hauled, with number *4* and seven coaches. It was a typical Dan run too. He managed a reasonable 51 mph at Whitehouse and then fell to 39–40 mph at both Bleach Green and Greenisland. Just 57 mph down the Mount was rather slow for Dan and the time to Carrickfergus of 15 m 27 s slightly lengthy, because of a relatively slow start to Seaview. We then managed 53 mph before Whitehead, reached in under seven and a half minutes. As usual, Dan would leave braking to the last possible moment, so the time of 3 m 57 s to Ballycarry, exceeding 48 mph, was quite good. On the section to Larne Town we just exceeded 48 mph before and 52 mph after traversing the slow loop at Magheramorne. Good starting and stopping kept the time down to a reasonable 10 m 33 s.

For the 19.15 homebound, the load was kept at seven coaches. Speeds of 38 mph, 40 mph and 48 mph were achieved on the three stopping sections to Glynn, Magheramorne and Ballycarry respectively. Up the hill to Whitehead we just managed 34 mph. We also took the eight minutes, all but a second, to Carrickfergus, with just 51 mph at Downshire Park. After Carrick Dan livened up again, managing 40 mph on the uphill section to Greenisland (reached in 5 m 59 s). We managed 45 mph before the Jordanstown stop (in 2 m 45 s) and 37 mph before Whiteabbey (in 2 m 32 s). In along the lough shore Dan managed 58mph at Post 2, before a signal stop outside the terminus increased the arrears to 11 minutes.

Paul and I were glad enough to head for home at a reasonably early hour, for that night there was even more widespread violence.

Thursday 14 August

Because of events I had got into the habit of turning on the radio each morning. Today there were reports of 'orchestrated' riots in many of the provincial towns – Strabane, Omagh, Dungannon, Armagh, Lurgan, Dungiven and Newry. As in Derry and Belfast, these had taken the form of Catholic youths in open battle with the Royal Ulster Constabulary. It appeared that law and order was breaking down and there were reports that the Home Secretary, James Callaghan, was on the brink of sending troops to the province. This turned out to be the case – before the day was out they had arrived in Derry, initially, and nobody could possibly have guessed how long they would stay.

Back at York Road, the same combination turned up on the 17.30 as on the previous evening. One could be dismissive – if it wasn't for the fact that this was to be my last ever steam run on the 17.30. As referred to below, in 'Last Things', the train was only ever steam-hauled on two occasions after this – both times with number *4*. A better start out to Seaview ensured that the first section to Carrickfergus was completed in 14 m 46 s. Dan exceeded 48 mph at Whitehouse, held 39 mph over Bleach Green, made 41–42 mph up to Greenisland and did not disappoint down the Mount, with a 61 mph maximum. Just under eight minutes to Whitehead without exceeding 50 mph was dull. So was just 38 mph before Ballycarry. But a slack on restarting from Ballycarry seemed to provide a little more motivation and we managed 50 mph before and just exceeded 54 mph after Magheramorne.

Again the load was held at seven coaches for the run home. Almost 40 mph before Glynn and a time of 3 m 46 s was bright work – though we got no more on to Magheramorne. At Magheramorne loop the hand tablet was dropped, wasting a couple of minutes, for we had to stop to retrieve this. After the unscheduled stop we just touched 49 mph. The run up to Whitehead was very weak, with only 32 mph. The section on to Carrickfergus proved a little better than the previous evening, with 53 mph at Downshire Park. Up through the Mount was very laborious, with only 34 mph at Trooperslane. Downhill was better, with 44 mph before Jordanstown and 39 mph before Whiteabbey, reached in a very sharp

2 m 29 s. Of course Dan kept the best till last! For what was my final section on a return 17.30, he managed 60 mph at Post 2 and would have been into York Road in six and a half minutes from Whiteabbey, had not a signal stop again impeded progress.

That night Belfast reverberated to the sound of gunfire.

Friday 15 August

The news was grim. Four people were dead, one a nine-year-old altar boy. They had been caught in gunfire between snipers and police. In the confusion, one side blamed the other and rumour flourished. The situation needed decisive action and that appeared in the form of a decision to send the army, only just arrived in Derry, to the streets of Belfast. Sporadic violence, particularly the burning and looting of premises, continued during the day.

In between news bulletins, the disc jockey played the songs of the moment. This was the month of 'Woodstock' and even the British hit parade had taken to folk rock. Particularly memorable were 'Marrakesh Express' and 'Si Tu Dois Partir'. So, while the dream that never was – Northern Ireland – fell apart before our eyes, teenage America strove valiantly to hold on to the 'American Dream'. Ultimately, they too would fail.

It was with some trepidation that I made my way to York Road, arriving there at just about 17.00 that evening. Given the circumstances, there was a reasonable turn out of enthusiasts, but conversation centred mostly on the day's events rather than on steam matters. I think we were all secretly relieved when an MPD set appeared on Platform 2 to work the 17.30. Had the train been steam-hauled we would have felt obliged to go, but that would have meant walking the route to Great Victoria Street at around 20.30 – and under the circumstances that was much too late to be around.

So we broke up and some of us returned to Great Victoria Street for connections on towards Lisburn. There, the sight could only be described as chaotic – like something I had only ever seen photographs of in books about World War Two. An hour after it was due to depart, the 17.30 'Enterprise Express' to Dublin still had not left. People who had friends or relatives in the Republic of Ireland had probably been encouraged to 'get out of Belfast' and something of a mini evacuation was under way. It was not until 18.50 that the 'Enterprise' eventually left, while the 18.35 semi-fast train to Dundalk (with a connection for Dublin) was hot on its heels at 18.56. The 18.45 local to Lisburn, in the hands of a three-car BUT set composed of power units *124* and *134* was consequently held until 19.00. Once away, we were signal checked almost immediately, which gave plenty of time to view the scene of destruction. Over to the right of the train, flames engulfed an old 'satanic mill' on the Grosvenor Road. The sky was dark and heavy with the smoke from this and other arson attacks further afield. It was one of the most frightening scenes I had, at that time, ever laid my eyes on and I was glad to be going home. At least Lisburn was, so far, unaffected by the mayhem.

Saturday 16 August

As on previous Saturdays, I arose early and headed to Lisburn station to catch the 06.40 ex-Portadown (due out of Lisburn at 07.07). I had been standing on the platform for nearly ten minutes when a BUT set appeared. It was not travelling at particularly high speed, but the driver sounded his horn and ran straight through. Then the story started to unfold. This was the train that left Dublin at 02.15 and only conveyed passengers beyond Portadown, where it was due to leave at 04.38. It then stopped at Lurgan and Lisburn only – the latter at 05.03. Its main purpose was to convey newspapers from the Dublin presses to Belfast, for distribution and sale. So it was affectionately called 'the newspaper train'. Until the closure of the Portadown to Derry line in 1965, this train had been steam-hauled. Some mornings, I would awake early and hear the comforting sound of a jeep (apparently *56* was a favourite for this turn) being worked hard out of Lisburn – often late and in a final bid to pick up a few minutes, for the precise running of this train depended upon when the presses were ready.

It had never been as late as it was on this morning though! With the reports of violence and destruction, the Dublin presses had been held for last minute reports and had rolled long into the night. Then, in an attempt to gain some time, the Lurgan and Lisburn stops were omitted, for the 06.40 local train was just a block or so behind. But the 06.40 had to make stops, so it was 07.28 before the six-car BUT set (power units *127*, *128* and *132*) left for Belfast.

I have an unnamed driver to thank that morning, for he only slacked at Lambeg, and by partially missing that stop he gained over a minute on the 20-minute schedule. As we pulled into Platform 4, I was already off the train and running towards the ticket barrier by the time it had come to a standstill. Now I was a trained runner, but the size of the task ahead of me was enormous. It was slightly under a mile and a half from the concourse of Great Victoria Street to the concourse of York Road station, and I had precisely eight minutes to be sure of making the 07.55 to Larne. In running kit and running shoes this would have been feasible, but I was dressed in jacket, trousers, walking shoes and carrying log books, watches and a camera! However, the adrenaline was pumping as I got under way in the pleasant morning summer sunshine – down Great Victoria Street, past the Grand Opera House, the ABC cinema, the 'Black Man', RBAI ('Inst') and the Belfast College of Technology; into King Street, across Castle Street and on through areas which today are part of the Castlecourt shopping complex; down Gresham Street and past the old Smithfield Market; and across North Street, where I turned left into the upper section of Royal Avenue. There wasn't another human being around, nor any cars or buses. Thankfully too, there was no sign of police or the newly arrived army, for the speed of my progress might have warranted some explanation! The grand clock above the Belfast Telegraph office registered nine

minutes to eight. I was halfway there in half the time, so there was still a chance of making it! More adrenaline pumped as I fled over Lower Donegall Street and passed the Co-operative building. There was no traffic to hold me at Frederick Street or Great George's Street. York Road and the Midland Hotel were now in sight. Passing a very quiet deserted Gallaher building, it was just another few hundred yards across the wide street and into the station concourse. Checking my watch, I discovered that I'd run the entire distance in five seconds under eight minutes – a pace of under five and a half minutes per mile!

There were no bands to greet me, nobody slung a medal around my shoulders or passed me an invitation to another race. But I had reward indeed, for the barrier gate into Platform 2 was still open. I breathlessly showed my ticket and proceeded to an open door in the six-coach set with ubiquitous engine number *5* at the head.

In fact Bobby Vance was a little over two minutes late away that morning – I could have taken it easier! He started well to Seaview, but then notched *5* up, managing only 42 mph before the Whiteabbey stop. The run up to Greenisland was better, with 38 mph before the stop in 5 m 28 s. Then there was more easy running, with only 46 mph through the Mount. We had an extra stop at Kilroot and a signal check before Whitehead, which rather ruined any chance of any running in from Carrickfergus. All the way *5* was repeatedly 'blowing off', so she clearly had no steaming problems. Then came a timid 39 mph before Ballycarry, though we did exceed 47 mph on the section to Magheramorne. Forty-two mph between Magheramorne and Glynn and 38 mph before the Town stop were no records, but Bobby was starting well from each stop, so the sectional times were generally better than the top speed suggested. We arrived at Larne Harbour just over eight minutes late. At least half of the additional lost time since leaving Belfast was due to the Kilroot stop and the signal check at Whitehead.

I had to make several attempts to get up from my seat – such was the acute muscle stiffness caused by the mammoth run to catch this train!

The run home was livelier – at least until signal checks ruined progress. Away just 25 minutes late, we exceeded 50 mph before Magheramorne and just touched 52 mph before the Ballycarry hand tablet exchange. Fifteen minutes to Milepost 15 was as good a start as you could expect for a return boat train, but then we were stopped at the Whitehead outer home signal. The 10:10 local from Whitehead to Belfast had been despatched in front of us and was not making good progress. So, when we got under way again Vance drove steadily, managing over 56 mph at Eden before more signals brought us to a further standstill at Carrickfergus. A fair start to Greenisland with 38–39 mph along the last stretch of uphill line was followed by more signal checks before Jordanstown, at Whiteabbey and again at Seaview. In between we again just exceeded 56 mph at Post 2. The delays were a pity, for this run had shown definite promise.

The last ever steam boat train to Larne left York Road at 14.07 that day, again with number 5 and six coaches, in the hands of driver Gordon Beggs of Larne. There were no fireworks, but a typical 14.05 run – 12 minutes to Greenisland, with just 46 mph at Whitehouse, 37 mph at Bleach Green and 38 mph up to the stop. A speed of 53 mph down the Mount was a little livelier than the morning's run. Just 51 mph before the Whitehead curves achieved a 'fair to middling' time of 7 m 40 s to this point. Thereafter we managed 44 mph before the Ballycarry stop and just 46 mph before Magheramorne. Almost 44 mph before Glynn was better and 38 mph before the Town was identical to the earlier run. The last steam 'down' boat train reached Larne Harbour just seven minutes late.

Another change of driver, before the final steam boat train left Larne Harbour just over half an hour late, put Bob Kemp back on the footplate. Sadly, this was a dire finale. The 17.20 stopping train had been despatched in front of us and Kemp knew rightly that if he ran hard he would be signal checked – so he didn't bother. The result was that we took over 19 minutes to an unscheduled stop in Whitehead – managed without exceeding 43 mph! Of greater interest were the expressions on the faces of holidaymakers who had just returned from Scotland and England. Two weeks ago they had left what apparently was a normal place, even if the undertow suggested otherwise. A short holiday later and what were they returning to – a war-torn province. Their questions were open with lots of what's and why's and how's. Their voices were quiet and deliberate and their faces were solemn, in deep consternation. The drab progress of the train merely formed a suitable backcloth.

After Whitehead, Kemp was marginally better – very marginally! We got away to just over 48 mph at Eden, but then the engine was allowed to drift back to below 30 mph at Greenisland. By this stage there was little chance of us catching the diesel in front, so Kemp just kept the setting on the engine unchanged and we ran away to 63 mph at Whitehouse. In all it was a dreadful run and yet we had still managed a respectable top speed – right at the death knell of steam hauled 'boat trains'.

Thursday 21 August 1997

All summer long the billboards had alerted us to the day. The 21 August had been sung and reverberated from the roof-tops. The BBC had run programmes in celebration of the music, articles had been written on the significance of the artwork, and hype had never had it so good! For this day heralded the release by Oasis of their follow-up album to the massive selling 'What's the story, Morning Glory'. It was unheard of to release an album on a Thursday – no doubt that also was to ensure that there were no other distractions.

That morning a young woman (though she could no longer be described as in her first flow of youth) was photographed as she elegantly jogged from her gym along the Earlscourt Road in London. She was not unaccustomed to that kind of attention, but ten days later she was dead, victim to a car accident in Paris. If Oasis thought they could stage-manage the biggest event of 1997, they had got it sadly wrong, for even arguably the best single from the album, 'Stand By Me', stood absolutely no chance of dislodging the tribute song to this woman from the UK (or any other) top slot.

Strangely, the album cover from 'Be Here Now' does not in any way depict 1997. Oasis are a band who lean heavily on late Beatles influence (particularly that of John Lennon). Not surprisingly, perhaps, the rather enigmatic album cover contains much rock memorabilia, dating back to the legends of the late 1960s – the Who, Eric Clapton and the Beatles. Even the timepiece looks like a clock from a Beeching-era railway station. The white Rolls Royce is reminiscent of the VW and John Lennon's suit on the cover of 'Abbey Road'. Its emersion in a swimming pool is a reminder of Brian Jones' untimely death. So I can be forgiven for thinking that the album cover, with its permanent calendar which distinctly says Thursday 21 August, might be indicating a different year – the year in which the events about to be described actually happened.

Thursday 21 August 1969

In 1969, 21 August was a Thursday. There were no banners, no advance programmes and no articles in the serious press to announce its coming. However, for a small group of people from East Antrim, it was at least a day set apart from usual. These people were the all too rapidly diminishing group who worked at the ICI factory at Kilroot, and this was the day of their annual outing to Portrush. Few, if any, of them probably realised, but they would be part of the privileged few to travel on the last 'company' steam-hauled train to Portrush. The next time a steam train reached this outpost, it would be firmly under the banner of preservation.

I had decided to meet the Larne portion of this train at Carrickfergus. This would ensure runs with at least two engines. To do this meant catching the 09.05 diesel from York Road. So I could have left Lisburn by the 08.23 semi-fast, but elected instead to take the earlier 08.12 – the

'angel in blue's' train. This act seemed to form some continuity between what was almost past and what was about to befall, and I guess that by this stage I had already resigned myself to the coming of autumn. September heralded a new academic year and maybe I was just reacquainting myself with one of the more pleasant aspects of that routine! So she and I made slow progress to Belfast, courtesy of a four-car BUT set with power cars *128* and *131*. The 09.05 from York Road was a three-car MPD set (power units *53* and *60*, with four-wheeled van) in rebellious form. Fortunately, the special steam train in from Larne Harbour was also late enough not to cause heart attacks in the subway at Carrickfergus!

It arrived – number *6*, oddly in bunk-first mode, driven by Tommy Dean and a large rake of nine coaches. This wasn't so funny for the Larne line, though Dean did his best, managing 30 mph before a stop in Greenisland, 49 mph before a further stop in Whiteabbey and finally just exceeding 50 mph in the lough shore, where a signal check at Seaview ensured that a couple more minutes were lost. There ended *6*'s passenger career, though she had probably been the least called upon engine in the year just past.

Maybe it was a sign of things to come in the textile and chemical industry of East Antrim, but there really were insufficient people to justify nine coaches. Poor *6* had had to struggle unnecessarily! The three coaches closest to her were detached, while *53* slipped down from the shed and coupled up to the remainder. The driver for the occasion was Peter McCann – an ex-Great Northern man and one capable of a thrilling run. With a little snitch of a load, our hopes were rising.

This seemed initially to be justified – over 51 mph at Whitehouse, holding 23 mph at Mossley was dull but alright. But once over Kingsbog, McCann notched *53* up so tightly she was hardly being worked at all. Running at only 56 mph at Doagh, he then shut off completely, allowing speed to fall to 44 mph at Muckamore. Thereafter he opened up again to attain the maximum of 58 mph (for the day) into the dip after Antrim. A speed of 49 mph was held over Post 26 and another 58 mph at Kellswater and we still held schedule into Ballymena. The run on to Ballymoney was similar. A good start up to Cullybackey, followed by a steady 40–41 mph up to Post 38 should have produced over 60 mph by Dunloy. Instead, we got just over 52 mph, with 58 mph down Ballyboyland. After Ballymoney we only managed 54 mph, before a very deliberately taken bridge slack and then just over 40 mph on the Portrush branch. This was dull timekeeping for a special train expected to have been taxed more heavily.

Everybody knew this was the end. There would never be another steam train to Portrush, special or timetabled, in NIR days. Without steam, Portrush would hold little attraction for us. It was the place we all loved to hate – a typical seaside town, full of 'tripperish' shops and penny arcades. The smell of burning rubber and electric sparks from the dodgems mingled with that of diesel from the generators, which supplied the other mechanical rides. Overwhelming was the pungent aroma of fish and chip shops, and the sight of people with soft ice cream cones from Morelli's. Then there were those two strands – the West and the East. There were few views that could compare with one's first sight of the former, as the train came over the hill, just a mile above the terminus. The more sheltered East Strand, with its blue lagoon, was pretty impressive too – and great for basking in when the sun shone! So we strode round the town, taking in sights that had held weekly familiarity, yet knowing it might be years before we ever came back again.

McCann and *53* returned in time for some of us (including Mac Arnold) to have a 'chat'. What had the problem been that morning? Didn't he know this really was the end? He listened to us sympathetically. "Problem is, lads, that *53* has a fallen brick-arch and to prevent further firebox damage we're having to run easily." Put simply, there was not going to be a grand finale.

We were due away at 18.25 and left almost

A double ending: 53's last passenger turn was also the final NIR steam train from Portrush on 21 August 1969.

dead on time. Accelerating to over 30 mph at Post 66, McCann did nothing more than 35 mph along the branch, before a signal check and eventual stop at Coleraine. There we sat for ten minutes while the 17.50 ex-Londonderry cleared the section. Then came another very tentative run over the slack and then a brighter 54 mph before another check and stop at Ballymoney. We sat there for nearly 15 minutes, awaiting a rather late 18.00 ex-York Road. This was certainly not the cleverest of paths!

The run up Ballyboyland was the best of a bad lot! Thirty-seven mph at the cabin was no record for six coaches, but what was nice was the fact that there was no minimum speed recorded. McCann continued to accelerate to Post 49 (39 mph) and just touched 45 mph before the Dunloy hand tablet exchange. Thereafter, *53* was eased and just managed 56 mph at Glarryford. Nevertheless, the even half hour time taken to stop in Ballymena (under yet another signal check) was probably better than schedule. Here we took water and then waited and waited for the road to clear.

Then news started to filter down the train. The 17.40 ex-Derry, which had been guilty of delaying us at Coleraine, was at it again! The train, in the hands of an MPD-set, had apparently smashed through closed level crossing gates just a mile on the Ballymena side of Antrim. The

An annual duty for the engines was to test the hydraulic buffer stops at York Road. No 5 is seen performing this task in January 1970.

leading car (*52*) had been damaged and it was now taking some time to clear the line of debris – and no doubt some unidentified steam engine had been called to the rescue! Even when we eventually got away from Ballymena, it was a case of proceeding with caution, under frequent signal checks and stops, and eventually creeping past the wrecked level crossing gates, now under hand signal control. So we got little more than 53 mph at Kellswater. There was a further signal stop at Antrim and even on the restart we were immediately checked. Clearly, the stricken 17.40 was not making swift progress.

It was a strange run up the bank once we did get going. McCann only managed 43 mph at Dunadry and we were down to 37 mph by the Airport Road crossing. Then he started to do enough to maintain speed in the low 40s – so that after an initial burst to 44 mph at Templepatrick, we ran the rest of the way to Kingsbog, in the now

fading light, at an almost constant 42 mph. "I can't give you a good run, but I'll be damned that it be described as completely bad!" Then we made nothing more than 53 mph at Mossley and a final run along the lough shore to stop in York Road at 21.41. It had taken three and a quarter hours to get home from Portrush.

As *53* reached the buffer-stop, that was it – the end of my steam dream, the end of innocence and childhood. Ahead, the route was charted differently. Ahead lay loss, regret and the pain of finally growing up. Much of the fall of '69 would, for me, be played out in a minor key, before a strange little event happened – but I must leave that to the epilogue.

The next day the Beatles posed for their last ever photo-call. And the band played on: 'Something in the way she moves, reminds me of no other lover...'

Last Things

After this, just ten passenger trains were intentionally steam-hauled. Sometimes there were unconfirmed reports of broken down diesels being rescued by steam, for as long as engines were involved in the 'spoil workings' (these did not end until 2 May 1970), but it was impossible to keep a record of every such occurrence. The 'ten' include that by number *4*, which had just hooked on to the 'Larne' end of the six coaches recently arrived from Portrush. She would take some very weary passengers home to Carrickfergus and Larne, about which an amusing story is told in *NCC Saga*. Of the remainder, six were Carrickfergus and Whitehead locals on Easter Monday and Tuesday 1970, and will presently be described. That leaves just three to be accounted for. On Saturday 6 September 1969, *50* worked her last passenger turn on a football special to Ballymena, producing a run that was as every bit as temperamental as we'd come to love and expect from her! Just two more 17.30s were steam-hauled – both with number *4* – on Thursday 28 August 1969 and Tuesday 9 September 1969. Enthusiast Stephen Rottger, who conveniently lived in a house overlooking the site of the old station at Whitehouse, noticed the last of these, heading out towards Larne. He made his way to Whiteabbey to meet the 19.15 return, and in so doing became the last enthusiast ever to record steam on a portion of the 17.30 or return.

Easter Monday 30 March 1970

Just 51 weeks separated Easter 1969 and Easter 1970. It was less than a year – and yet the change of mood as I stood at York Road could not have been more poignant. In the intervening months there had been a lot of changes. I had lost my grandfather, and at 17 it was probably the first time I'd really dealt with loss. I'd reached the age of 'consent' and would cast my first vote in a by-election in just a few weeks time. The 'angel in blue' and I were now on speaking terms – even if subject matter never progressed beyond the weather. She would ultimately 'fade to blue', while others took her place. I'd also just met a girl called Lorraine – though we were just good friends – at least that was what I kept telling my mother, when scented green and mauve envelopes dropped through the letterbox of our new abode in Dunmurry (near Milepost 108)! In school I'd been made a prefect and would complete A' levels in less than three months time. In musical taste I'd progressed from singles to albums! Altogether, I'd grown up and (sadly?) turned just a tiny bit more serious.

NIR scarcely needed steam for what was a cold, inclement holiday period. All Portrush specials were composed of diesels or diesels hauling steam coaches (some of which had been decoratively repainted in a fine maroon colour). During the winter, two more engines had succumbed, to never again move under their own steam. Not surprisingly, one was number *10*, but

(Continued on page 121)

Ex-SLNCR 0-6-4T No 27 Lough Erne *heads towards York Road after picking up a consignment of sleepers in Belfast Docks on 8 August 1969.*

JA Cassells

The 6.05 special! With passenger turns all but finished, stone trains and line maintenance became the only role for the surviving engines. No 53 is seen passing Whitehouse with a crane special to Londonderry on 23 August 1969.

JA Cassells

After arriving with the 15.35 from York Road on 30 March 1970, No 4 runs round its train at Whitehead.

Author

A few minutes later No 4 is shunting its maroon coaches into the 'excursion' siding at Whitehead to clear the way for two other trains to cross at Whitehead station, before No 4 departs on the 16.38 to Belfast. A year later, Whitehead excursion station was to become the permanent home of No 4 in preservation.

Author

On the final day of steam passenger operations, 31 March 1970, engine 4 is seen running round the 15.05 to York Road at Carrickfergus.

Author

A down empty stone train, headed by No 4 and banked by No 51, drifts into Whitehead on 6 August 1969. The stone trains ran for nearly four years in connection with the building of the M2/M5 along the loughshore at Belfast With four (at one point five) lanes in each direction, the M2/M5 was the widest motorway in the British Isles.

CP Friel

The scene at Magheramorne on 2 May 1970. The final stone train is about to be hauled by No 53, whilst a 'Hampshire' unit has conveyed NIR guests to the event.

Norman Johnston

The final stone train from Magheramorne, with 53 at the head and 4 at the rear, passes Whitehead Golf Club on 2 May 1970.

Norman Johnston

After stone trains finished, two jeeps continued to perform station pilot duties: 4 and 51 are seen here at York Road on 22 May 1970.

Norman Johnston

(Continued from page 116)

the other was former summer hero *50*. That left just six 'in traffic'. The deteriorating mechanical condition of all remaining engines was the final nail in the coffin of mainline steam. So, during Easter 1970, the limited diesel shortages that still existed were dealt with by rostering just six Carrickfergus and Whitehead local steam – four on Monday and two on Tuesday.

Somehow three coaches (in the new maroon livery) on the Larne line just didn't have the appeal of a big train to Portrush. I was merely there to record the very final death knell of passenger steam operations in the British Isles, and that is unfair because some of the work on these little trains was great. Shed favourite number *4* worked all of the trains but one. Driver Jackie Kitchen and fireman T McCrum were clearly enjoying themselves on the 09.50 to Carrickfergus. Despite a permanent way check

at Fortwilliam, we still managed 54 mph at Whitehouse. A speed of 36 mph was attained on both sections to Jordanstown and Greenisland. Down the hill we managed 46 mph on the short (less than one and a fifth miles) section to Trooperslane and 49 mph before the Clipperstown stop, almost one and a half miles further down the hill. This was comparable to what a 450-class unit might produce today (if it didn't fail!). The 10.23 return from Carrick was in similar vein. Most noteworthy was 34 mph between Trooperslane and Greenisland, 45 mph before Jordanstown and 59 mph along the lough shore (after a sub-two minute start through Whitehouse). Enthusiast Norman Foster was so encouraged by steam in a new decade, that he tried to stretch this to 'the first 60 in 70', but I'm afraid it eluded me!

The 12.35 to Carrick was another smartly worked affair. This time we managed 56 mph at Whitehouse in a smart seven-minute time to

The 09.50 local to Carrickfergus, headed by No 4, at Greenisland on 30 March 1970. Note the newly applied NIR logo on the freshly painted carriage.

The 12.35 local to Carrickfergus leaving Clipperstown halt behind No 4 on 30 March 1970.

The same engine and train worked the 15.35 local to Whitehead, seen here at Jordanstown.

The 15.35 local to Whitehead passing Kilroot with No 4 on 30 March 1970.

Whiteabbey. Also notable was 38 mph between Jordanstown and Greenisland and almost 50 mph between Trooperslane and Clipperstown. The 13.20 return produced very good uphill work, with 32 mph between Clipperstown and Trooperslane and over 35 mph on to Greenisland. Just over two and a half minutes and almost 46 mph before Jordanstown would also stand any modern comparison.

The 15.35 to Whitehead was Jackie's final steam passenger turn and was a magnificent finale. Despite the permanent way check, we again attained 56 mph at Whitehouse and produced another 38 mph between Jordanstown and Greenisland. Between Trooperslane and Clipperstown 52 mph and a time of 2 m 36 s is probably beyond most 450-class and 80-class three-car units. From the little staggered one-coach platform at Eden to Whitehead took just 5 m 40 s, with top speed 54 mph and a signal check just outside the destination. The 16.38 return was even better. Particularly notable was 37 mph on the three-quarter mile stretch

between Eden and Downshire Park, 37 mph between Clipperstown and Trooperslane and almost 39 mph on the next section on to Greenisland. These statistics would be well beyond current three-car unit capability. And what about 49 mph between Greenisland and Jordanstown (time 2 m 31 s)! Of course Norman was eventually proved right – we definitely got the '60 in 70' after Whitehouse, on the final section in from Whiteabbey.

At Belfast there was no time to run round the train before the 17.35 departed, so number 5, with driver Willie McAleese and fireman Joe Magill, simply coupled on the other end. In doing so 'first of the class' 5 worked its last passenger train but, unlike No 4 the following day, was to end up in the cutter's yard. Running was not as bright, but we did manage 49 mph between Kilroot and Whitehead. But the 18.15 return was better, with 50 mph before a signal check at Kilroot. A speed of 39 mph between Eden and Barn was quite good too, as was 33 mph between Clipperstown and Trooperslane

No 5's last passenger duty. She is preparing to leave Whitehead with the 18.15 to York Road on 30 March 1970.

and 34 mph on to Greenisland. Another two-minute start out of Whiteabbey to Whitehouse and just over 56 mph before permanent way slacks took their toll. It was hard to believe that within days this engine would never function again, but the following Friday I watched her pass Milepost 108 (close to where I had just relocated), with a Great Northern ballast train as her final duty.

Easter Tuesday 31 March 1970

For the final day of steam passenger operations in the British Isles, there were just two Larne line locals, both in the hands of soon-to-be preserved number *4* and a driver who, the previous summer, had witnessed the end of steam in the maiden city – Davie McDonald. He was assisted by fireman George Robinson. Nothing of note was managed on the 14.35 local to Carrickfergus. On the 15.05 return we again exceeded 32 mph between Clipperstown and Trooperslane and managed 56 mph after Whitehouse, before permanent way and signal checks.

The 16.40 to Whitehead was brighter, with 43 mph between Greenisland and Trooperslane, 47 mph on to Clipperstown and over 50 mph between Eden and Whitehead.

The last 'company'-operated passenger steam train in the British Isles left Whitehead five minutes late at half past five on a cool Easter Tuesday, 1970. On this turn the section on to Carrickfergus was littered with request slacks and stops, but we still exceeded 50 mph before Kilroot. We also ran non-stop from Clipperstown to Greenisland, with a top speed of 43 mph in 5 m 23 s – a feat certainly beyond modern diesel units such as *453* and *455*! After another 46 mph before Jordanstown and almost 58 mph after Whitehouse, the last ever passenger steam train came to a halt in York Road at 18.05. At least tonight there was a silver lining. The engine now arriving would not be departing for the knacker's yard. Soon *4* would become the property of the RPSI and hopefully will be back in steam soon in the twenty-first century. Who knows, maybe one day they'll run

No 4 leaving Clipperstown for Belfast with the 15.05 ex-Carrickfergus on 31 March 1970, the last day of steam passenger working.

The same train arriving at Trooperslane just over three minutes later.

A moment in railway history! This, rather than BR's famous 'Fifteen Guinea Special' of 11 August 1968, was the last company-operated steam passenger train in the British Isles (apart from BR's narrow gauge Vale of Rheidol line). No 4 approaches Carrickfergus with the 17.25 ex-Whitehead on 31 March 1970. Unlike the 'Fifteen Guinea Special', you could have travelled on the last steam train from Whitehead for 3s 9d (18p)!

It's all over now. In contrast to the crowds who watched the last steam train in Britain, a comparatively small group of enthusiasts greet the arrival of 4's final passenger turn in 'NIR' days. Facing the engine from the left are Alex Lindsay, Robert White and the author. Driver Davie McDonald is on the footplate.

her on lightly loaded stopping trains, just to show what these engines could do on local turns – assuming of course that NIR first get the necessary finance to fix the track!

Just over a month later, on Saturday 2 May 1970, the operation that had kept steam going so valiantly during the previous summer came to an end. The last 'spoil train' (complete with headboards detailing the total number of 'stone trains' that had run in the four years since the contract had started) was hauled up from Magheramorne, by engines *53* and *4* (see pages 119 and 120).

Two engines, *4* and *51*, survived at York Road for some months afterwards, generally performing station pilot duties. So, steam remained on a UK mainline railway until late 1970; but for me the sight was just too hard to bear.

Epilogue

08:36 hrs: Monday 24 November 1969

The four-car BUT set, forming the 07.45 ex-Portadown, made a spirited entry to Belfast's Great Victoria Street station – too spirited in fact, for as driver Jimmy Sneddon made the final brake application, the response from cars *124* and *133* was not quite timely enough. With speed modestly down to below walking pace, we struck the buffers and with that impact I struck gold! For this was sufficient to upend some passengers in car *124*, who were already on their feet and waiting to dismount on to Platform 2. I fortunately managed to hold my balance and caught one unfortunate young woman as she toppled over and what a catch! What would I not have given to hold, even for a fleeting second, the 'angel in blue' in my arms? That crack on the buffers broke the ice and, even if my first spoken words to her were banal in the extreme, as I underwent an attack of acute embarrassment, in that one small moment were established, between us, two of the most important ingredients of any relationship – communication and recognition.

I think she recognised my predicament, but she always dealt softly with me. Soon a smile or a word of greeting would become common place and if the relationship never developed any further – well, it was never meant to. But with each smile or each "Hello", I was flung, fast forwards, on a trip to paradise. Slowly, very slowly, I even started to believe in myself. But then all this came long afterwards – long after the summer of 1969...